paint
saves the day

CREATIVE
HOMEOWNER®

paint
saves the day

Lucianna Samu
Photography by Mark Samu

CREATIVE HOMEOWNER®, Upper Saddle River, New Jersey

PAINT SAVES THE DAY

SENIOR EDITOR	Kathie Robitz
SENIOR GRAPHIC DESIGNER	Glee Barre
JUNIOR EDITOR	Angela Hanson
PHOTO COORDINATOR	Mary Dolan
DIGITAL IMAGING SPECIALIST	Frank Dyer
INDEXER	Schroeder Indexing Services
COVER DESIGN	Glee Barre
FRONT & BACK COVER PHOTOGRAPHY	Mark Samu

CREATIVE HOMEOWNER

VICE PRESIDENT AND PUBLISHER	Timothy O. Bakke
ART DIRECTOR	David Geer
MANAGING EDITOR	Fran J. Donegan
PRODUCTION COORDINATOR	Sara M. Markowitz

Current Printing (last digit)
10 9 8 7 6 5 4 3 2 1

Paint Saves the Day, First Edition
Library of Congress Control Number: 2008943781
ISBN-10: 1-58011-457-1
ISBN-13: 978-1-58011-457-8

Manufactured in the United States of America

CREATIVE HOMEOWNER®
A Division of Federal Marketing Corp.
24 Park Way
Upper Saddle River, NJ 07458
www.creativehomeowner.com

dedication

This book is dedicated to Lee, Pam, Eileen, Gary, and especially

Steven H., for their many years of cheerful camaraderie and profes-

sional know-how, which they unselfishly shared with me along the

way. A special thanks to Peter, for his unwavering support.

acknowledgments

My sincere thanks to Deidre Gatta of Artistic Designs by Deidre.

Not only an extraordinarily fine artist and decorative painter, but

also a dear friend, whose help and inspiration with this project has

been immeasurable.

contents

introduction

The intent of this book is to offer you fresh and practical ideas on adding beauty to your surroundings and tackling some tricky decorating problems by using spirited color and sensible paint solutions.

Inspiring photographs and reliable step-by-step instructions will bolster your confidence and help you to identify and formulate your own personalized color palette for decorative painting techniques.

Once the exclusive domain of faux finishers and accomplished artisans, color washing, wall glazing, texturing techniques, and even Venetian plastering are now skills every novice can learn to master, thanks in part to reliable, premixed glazing formulas and user-friendly products and tools. With know-how and reliable product resources, your ability to expertly transform problem floors, embellish simple tag-sale furniture, and add whimsy and charm to your most daunting decorating challenges will be a snap using faux marbling, stenciling, or simple freehand patterns. Soon, you'll be lavishing your dreary laundry room with a stunning color wash, brightening your closet interiors with smashing combinations, and painting your way to design chic every time you pry open a can of paint.

Most of the projects are shown as the work progressed in real-life situations to solve real-life problems, rather than sample boards in a controlled studio situation. You will see how architectural anomalies, walls in poor condition, and dated cabinets are transformed into design features of merit. With a few dollars and a little imagination, *Paint Saves the Day* offers solutions for rescuing inferior furnishings, outdated art pieces, and sorry little accessories, in addition to showing you how thrift-store finds and garage-sale cast-offs can become

PAINT A WOOD FLOOR? Yes! It's not difficult and it's a stylish alternative to traditional staining, as well as a solution for old wood floors that can't be refinished.

snappy, stylish accessories.

Many years of experience as a decorative painter have left me quite fearless when it comes to paint; it's cheap; it's readily available in a gazillion colors; it stores well; it can be manipulated into beguiling faux finishes; it's available in myriad emulsions and sheens; and it can be made to last and endure on practically any surface known to man.

Whether you're an aspiring faux finisher, a fanatical do-it-yourselfer, or an uneasy beginner, with *Paint Saves the Day* you too will fearlessly create your own beautifully painted accessories, surfaces, and stunningly beautiful rooms.

You may call home a tiny apartment, spare and functional, or maybe it's a big old house loaded with character. Whichever, creating a comforting retreat that suits your personality and lifestyle is an exhilarating pursuit. Your home is more than just a place to hang your hat, and you probably demand a lot of it. It has to be a place for

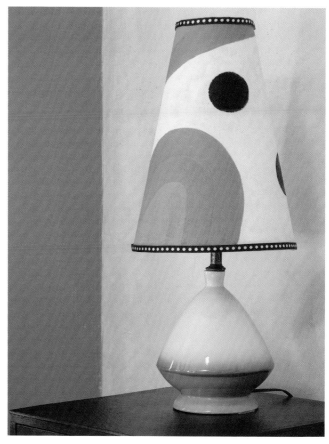

CUSTOMIZE A LAMPSHADE with paint. It's certainly less expensive than buying a new one, especially if it's an unusual shape or size.

relaxation, recreation, and rest. It requires room for work, spaces dedicated specifically to the needs of children, pets, guests, and personal pursuits.

"Home" in today's world is not only a refuge but also a source of inspiration where you can stylishly live your life. As you endeavor to make your corner of the world functional, your instinct to add your own personality and embellishments is natural. *Paint Saves the Day* will help.

the Classics

you can always count on these techniques

to make the ordinary extraordinary

The popularity of **decorative painting techniques** has grown to epic proportions. It is a life's work to explore every color combination, layering scenario, and tool option, so I've presented the fundamental methods of **glazing, washing, dragging, sponging, ragging,** and Venetian plaster in this first chapter. I recommend painting samples, which will help to expand your color horizons and build your skill and your **confidence with using the tools** and **mixing a suitable glaze.** The real challenge—and beauty—of each technique comes alive under the brush or tool of a less-studied or even unorthodox approach. **Practice** may not make perfect, but it can be interesting!

A VENETIAN PLASTER treatment brought color, texture, and personality into a contemporary room that had few outstanding architectural features.

Mixing a Glaze 1, 2, 3

Many techniques acquire their unique character with glazes and washes, and like today's array of tools, there is an equal number of opinions for executing a perfectly glazed surface. Glaze adds a wonderful atmospheric depth to a painted wall surface. Depending on the tool and the glaze formula, you can create a cottage-style color wash, sophisticated strié, whimsical broken color, or elegant, understated stipple.

types of glazes

Off-the-shelf proprietary glazing liquids include both alkyd (oil-based) and latex (water-based) formulations. There are several less-than-subtle differences between them, chiefly the drying time. The longer a glaze takes to dry, the more time and care you can give to manipulating it. Much like master chefs hoarding their culinary secrets, professional decorative artists have historically guarded any useful formula that would extend the drying time of their mixed glazes. Some have even been known to camouflage the additive's container in order to keep things under wraps on a project! It may appear that this conceit gave finishers a nonchalant attitude, but the long "open time" (meaning the glaze is still wet enough for you to manipulate it with a tool) is essential if the walls are large or the finish requires a lot of manipulation. For these reasons, you can use the easier-to-clean, less-toxic latex alternatives. However, none of these options will stay open as long as old-fashioned oil glaze, particularly when it's been "juiced up" with additives that slow down drying.

Purists and old timers may disagree about whether modern latex glazes are good alternatives to oil glazes. They may be right; the finish is softer, and these glazes dry quicker. They lack the body of oil glazes, and some can be finicky about accepting a tint. Still, with a little bit of tinkering, the more user-friendly products can produce dazzling effects.

The glaze formulas that follow are meant to provide a general idea of ratios and proportions. Knowing that paint will add body, thinning will increase transparency, and mixing and matching colors using paint or tint will alter the result, you are free to fool around with the formulas to your heart's delight. Seeing how far a glaze can be pushed, or thinned, while still holding the desired pattern is every decorative painter's obsession. But remember, the thinner the glaze, the quicker it dries. How fast can you work?

be a pro

OIL-SOAKED and glaze-laden rags can be a serious safety hazard because they can spontaneously combust. These rags generate heat as they dry. So when you've finished using them, rinse the rags in a bucket of soapy water and allow them to dry outside before attempting to dispose of them. In addition, DO NOT place oil-soaked rags inside tightly sealed trash bags.

THIS MONOCHROMATIC ROOM (left) looks serene in muted shades of blue. A tinted glaze, mixed to match the room's soft furnishings, adds depth to the walls.

SUNNY BUT SOFT YELLOW (below) evokes the warmth of a house in southern Italy. When you're tinting a glaze, play with the color to get it right. Try it on a board and see how both natural and artificial light affect its appearance in the room that you are painting.

Transparent Alkyd-Glaze Formulas

Glazing liquid	Solvent	Tint	Advantages/disadvantages
4 parts	4 parts	universal tint	A basic general-purpose glaze formula for tooled or ragging, or sponging-off techniques. The glaze will be quite transparent, owing to its lack of paint. Increase the solvent to as much as 8 parts for a thinner glaze.
4 parts	1 part	universal tint	Heavier than a basic glaze, and still quite transparent without the paint, this is a nice mix for a rubbed, applied rag or sponge technique, and negative paper and plastic manipulations, such as frottage.
4 parts	1 part	1 part alkyd paint	This is a heavy glaze that will not level up or disappear under the brush. Use this for fine strié, brushed plaids, more-opaque negative methods, and very high work.
4 parts	2 parts	2 parts oil-based enamel	Less transparent than the basic glaze, this one will not sag, stays open the longest, and dries to the highest sheen. You can add universal tint to it, as well as an additive to keep it workable longer.

To extend the open, or dry time, of alkyd-glaze formulas, reduce the solvent in any of the above formulas by 25 percent, replacing it with one of the following:

- Poppy-seed oil
- Walnut oil
- Boiled linseed oil
- Alkyd paint conditioner
- Linseed stand oil

The resulting glaze formulas will have an open time of about 30 minutes, depending on the temperature of the room and the wall surface. If the heat or the air conditioner is on full blast, you'll lose about 10 minutes. All of these oils will become amber or somewhat yellow. The poppy seed oil, which is the most expensive type, becomes the least amber; the linseed stand oil will shine and will become the most amber.

DRYING TIME is a major consideration when you're applying a glaze, especially if you're working alone or on a large wall. Most furniture pieces do not pose a problem, however.

A TWO-COLOR LATEX WASH in a vibrant cobalt and a Prussian blue lifts the spirits of this bathroom niche. The washes are applied over an existing mid-sheen beige paint. (See "Washes" on page 20.)

Transparent Latex-Glaze Formulas

Glaze	Water	Tint	Advantages/disadvantages
4 parts	2 parts	universal tint	A basic general-purpose glaze formula for tooled or ragging, or sponging-off techniques. The glaze will be quite transparent, owing to its lack of paint. Increase the solvent (water) by as much as you can control for a thin glaze.
4 parts	1 part	universal tint	Heavier than a basic glaze, and still quite transparent without the paint, this is a nice mix for a color wash, applied rag or sponge technique, and negative paper or plastic manipulations, such as frottage.
4 parts	1 part	2 parts latex paint	This is a heavy glaze that will not level up or disappear under the brush. Use this for fine strié, brushed plaids, more-opaque negative methods, and very high work.
4 parts	2 parts	2 parts high-gloss latex enamel	Less transparent than the basic glaze, this glaze will not sag, stays open the longest, and dries to the highest sheen. You can add more color with a universal tint.
4 parts	4 parts	gouache, universal tints	An entirely transparent, highly color-saturated color-wash formula that will dry powdery.

The 4 parts glaze/4 parts water formula is the mix to which the following additives can be introduced to extend the open time.
- Additive
- Glycerin
- Liquid dish-washing detergent
- Latex paint conditioner

a scumble glaze

The term "scumble glaze," whether it's an oil- or water-based formula, refers to the color of the glaze and not the glaze formula itself. Otherwise called an "overglaze," or a "veil," a scumble is always a lighter color than the glaze over which you apply it. It will always soften the underlying effect and is quite useful to fix a less-than-perfect glazing result. The more paint a scumble glaze formula contains, the more opaque the veil. Keep in mind the glazed surface must be completely dry before you apply a scumble over it. Otherwise, the scumble will activate the glazed layer. To play it safe, allow a minimum of an overnight dry. If you are in a hurry, layer incompatible mediums over one another or reduce the solvent in the scumble by half.

Glazing, a Master Class

After you have mixed a glaze, it's time to explore the limitless effects you can create by manipulating it with various tools and brushes. The examples here will give you some idea of how you can create different patterns in the glaze, but add your own interpretations and tools to the mix.

More often than not, the tool you choose to work the glaze will define the technique. To that end, it's useful to know how to hold the tool or brush and move it about the glaze to create the desired effect. These manipulations and the resulting wall finish will be created by your hand or a specific method. Here are a few things to keep in mind, especially if this is your first attempt.

- **Work on one wall at a time.** Tape the corners. Don't work around the perimeter of a room, but skip across to an opposing wall, then to a small niche, and so forth. This random approach to the entire room will actually help the final result appear more consistent.
- **Your hand, arm, legs, and back** will grow tired as a day of glazing wears on. This will have a considerable effect on your result. Start out on the small surfaces until you have a good fix on your stamina. A tired painter's hand removes far less glaze than that of a fleet early bird.
- **Before you begin a large, long wall,** be sure you can stay with it until you reach the other end. Have your ladder, staging, and tools at the ready and be sure your drop cloths, tape, and anything else that will cause you to stop are all in perfect order. Have your lunch, take the phone off the hook, and visit the restroom. Get everything set and go, go, go.
- **Your glazing style** will not match that of any helpers. If you are lucky enough to have help, work together in a sort of over-and-under one another arrangement. Or one can apply the glaze, while the other can work the tool and create the technique. Don't divvy up the room into sections—this will rarely work for beginners. In time, and with the same helper, you can each learn to create similar patterns, but this takes patience and practice.

Washes

Unlike a glaze, a wash is made up of thinned latex paint. An even thinner wash consists of a bucket of water, a little dish soap, a dollop of latex paint, and a universal tint. But the

basic scumble-glaze formula

- 4 parts glazing liquid
- 6 parts solvent or water*

TINT
Choose a basic latex formula for your scumble if you want a flat finish, or a basic oil-glaze formula for more sheen.

* Refer to "Transparent Alkyd-Glaze Formulas," on page 16 and "Transparent Latex-Glaze Formulas," on page 19.

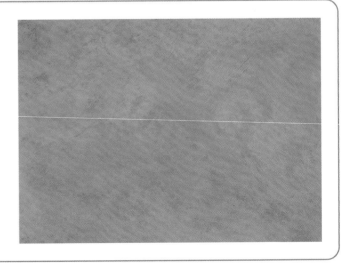

UNLIKE A LATEX GLAZE, **which can look dry and dusty, an oil glaze applied over a textured wall appears luminous. Its rich density implies a surface that has mellowed with age. The Naples yellow oil-glazed texture here will continue to gain depth over time.**

thinnest wash is called a "gouache," which is mixed with watercolors. You'll need to be fast with a brush and confident in your technique when you're applying a wash.

The ground, or base coat, could be an eggshell finish for a thinned paint wash, a flat latex for a water wash, or a textured wall surface, which will accept either one quite nicely.

Vibrant colors and any colors that you consider ugly or boring can all be changed quickly and dramatically with a wash. It's good to keep in mind that often the more vibrant base-coat colors result in the most exciting final finishes.

Make a sample, or experiment on an inconspicuous wall to see what kind of magic happens before you commit to an entirely new painting project. Just remember that because a wash is transparent, it will not conceal the color of the base coat entirely. But use the technique to your advantage, especially where you want to add drama where it's needed.

be a pro

MAKING A SAMPLE

Samples can be produced on oak tag, bristol board, foam core, or drywall. Each will need to be primed. Prime bristol board, foam core, and oak tag (the shiny side) with an oil-based product; you can use a latex primer on cut drywall. Acrylic craft paint is an inexpensive alternative to latex paint for a perfectly suitable sample-making base coat. Or practice your color-mixing talents with universal tints and a can of latex paint. If you wish to try repeated applications of an oil glaze and will be applying and removing the glaze on a single sample board, use oil-based primer and paint, which will hold up to this treatment the best.

color washing

Use the largest brush you feel comfortable holding. A 4-inch chip brush is almost perfect, but a 6-inch stain brush is even better. Apply a good amount of glaze to the surface in random crisscross strokes, overlapping as you go, until the brush is quite dry **(figure 1)**. The end result will be soft if you continue to work the glaze with brush strokes **(figure 2)**.

Figure 1

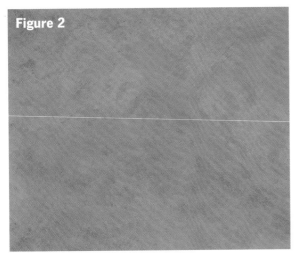

Figure 2

frottage with paper

Apply the glaze to the wall with a brush or short nap roller. (It's easier to distribute the glaze evenly with a brush.) Press newspaper, plain white paper, or kraft paper into the glazed surface and soften it with your open hand **(figure 3)**. Remove the paper and reposition it again on another section of the wet glaze. Move around the wall a bit with the paper, which will lose its ability to create a pattern after about three or four applications. Use a fresh sheet as you move to the next area, and repeat the process, turning the paper this way and that for a random look **(figure 4)**.

Figure 3

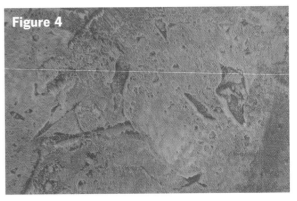

Figure 4

Figure 5

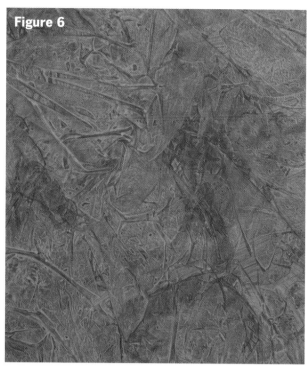

Figure 6

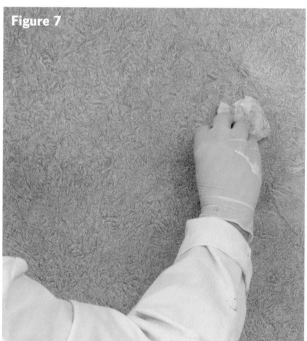

Figure 7

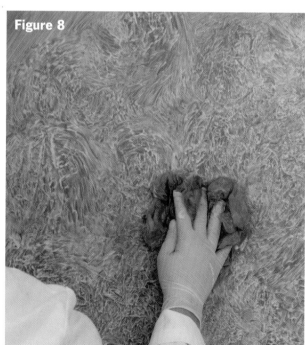

Figure 8

creating patterns with plastic

Every type of tool affects glaze differently and every type of plastic has a character of its own. Nothing beats dry-cleaning plastic, which can be laid onto large expanses of wall and removed to reveal a truly unbelievable textured surface **(figures 5 & 6)**. Small plastic bags and sheet plastic are generally less soft, and they leave a more angular and sharp pattern in the glaze. You can also stipple (pounce) a wall with a small piece of scrunched-up plastic; the plastic sold in rolls seems to be best for this **(figures 7 & 8)**. Although it's a time-consuming method, it's a handsome technique for dark glazes, and especially useful for an awe-inspiring red-glazed wall.

vertical strié with a brush

It's common to try to steady a brush by keeping a finger, or specifically a thumb, over the ferrule. This makes for a very tired wrist, to say nothing of the finger, in no time. It's better to hold the brush as you would a microphone, fingers wrapped around the handle, thumb closed over the top **(figure 9)**. Lean on the brush with your arm to keep the work straight. You'll last a lot longer this way, and you can snap a few lines here and there or have a helper hold a straightedge to keep your lines plumb **(figure 10)**.

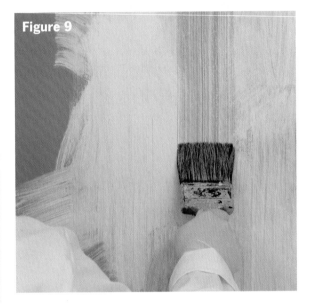

Figure 9

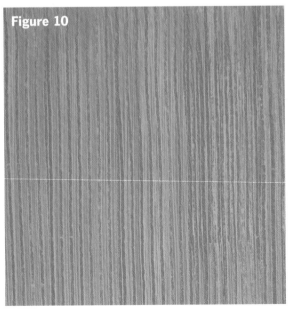

Figure 10

horizontal strié with a brush

You will not be able to brace your arm as easily moving side to side, nor hold the brush in the same manner as you would for a vertical strié. With practice, you can lay the brush between your thumb and forefinger with virtually no grip if you press the weight of all of your fingers over the bristles and press the brush into the glaze as you move across the wall **(figure 11)**. Line up each row evenly **(figure 12)**.

Figure 11

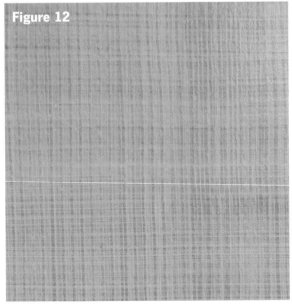

Figure 12

HELLO HANDSOME! Refinishing a piece of furniture can restore luster and style to a piece. Note the good-looking inlaid effect created on this console by dragging a brush in a different direction in alternate "panels" on the door.

design consult

If you must stop in the middle of a wall, the glaze will set up and no amount of skill or prayers will erase the line that will appear between glazing sessions. There are two solutions for this, however.

First, make the best blend you can, and over-glaze the entire wall with a paler scumble. (See page 20.)

Second, remove the completed, somewhat dry area with a ton of rags and the appropriate solvent, which is paint thinner for oil glazing. Such fiascos are the bane of everyone who has ever gotten "stuck" in the middle of the wall, but you can be sure that you will never allow anyone to interrupt your work again.

horizontal texture with a wallpaper brush

Years of experience has proven to me that the softer the grip on the tool, the longer the wrist will last. Any time you can develop a style that uses the strength of all the fingers, the less stress any one finger will suffer. Keep the hand relaxed, and use the strength of your arm to do the work **(figure 13)**. This technique produces a tight-grain wood look **(figure 14)**.

Figure 13

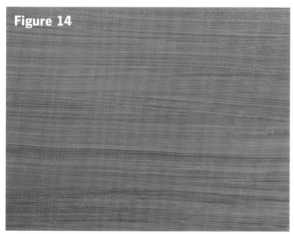

Figure 14

tooled patterns with a notched squeegee

Hold the squeegee using the same microphone grip and locked arm combination described in "Vertical Strié with a Brush." (See page 24.) Pull it down through the glaze in one long motion **(figure 15)**. Plan how you'll get up and down the ladder, too, if you are working on a full-height wall. Clean the glaze from the squeegee after each run using a dry rag.

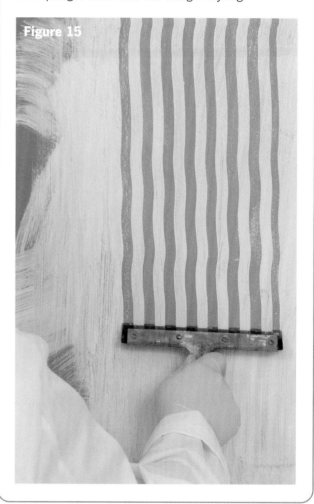

Figure 15

IT'S HARD TO GROW BORED with a beautifully executed, understated strié. This technique is timeless, especially in a period home with handsome trimwork. Here, the choice of a dark beige base coat and a pale, nearly white glaze adds to the overall subtlety of the result.

be a pro

SAVVY SQUEEGEE WORK

When you're applying a combed technique to a tall surface using a notched rubber sqeegee, mount the tool on a 2-foot extension pole. This will allow you to step back as you drag the squeegee through the glaze. This method also makes it easier to create reasonably straight strokes, as well as continuous ones.

combing with a rubber comb

Hold the comb, all fingers on top, and drag it through the glaze in one soft motion **(figure 16)**.

Figure 16

be a pro

EXPERT CORNERS AND CLEAN EDGES are what separate the pro from the novice when it comes to glazing a wall. To get a corner perfect, tape the adjoining wall top to bottom, and work your way into or out of it. Apply less glaze than you would on an open wall area, and move it into the corner using a small brush. If you are working with a special tool or brush to create a pattern, wait until you get a small amount of glaze in the corner and at the edge with the brush. Then you can go over it, manipulating the glaze as you like. Remember, it's always better to err on the side of too little glaze and too little pattern.

mottling with a sea sponge

Always begin by soaking a clean sponge in water until it's saturated. Then wring it out completely before giving it a good dunk into the glaze. "Clean" the sponge with a dry rag or newspaper. Now you're ready; pick up some glaze with the sponge, offloading a bit onto the rag or paper. Begin applying the remaining glaze to the wall in a soft, even-handed technique. Don't pinch the sponge; wrap your entire hand around it, twisting and turning your hand and wrist as you work randomly over the wall **(figures 17 and 18)**. Remember that a clean tool or sponge makes a different imprint than a glaze-laden one—so clean or blot it after each dip into the glaze.

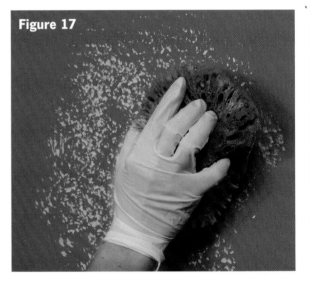

Figure 17

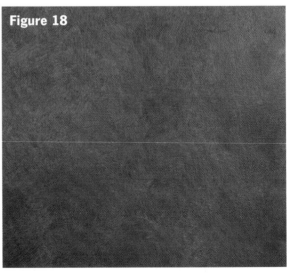

Figure 18

PRETTY IN PINK, the walls in this ultra-formal sitting room might appear out of place were
it not for the glaze, which lends a thoughtful and stately air to a whimsical color.

RENDERING TRADITIONAL OIL-GLAZING TECHNIQUES in familiar colors inspired by natural pigments creates an Old World feeling. Varying the tone of the yellow ochre, burnt sienna, and raw sienna glaze into a monochromatic three-color technique suggests a little age and wear.

rubbing with a rag

I arrived late to this party, but I find the motion of simply rubbing a glaze over a wall so pleasing that it's nearly therapeutic. I would not recommend it for very high walls unless the colors are so sympathetic that a hole here or there will not detract from the finish and send you looking for the solvent. Soft T-shirts work well for this, and I'm especially fond of the results well-worn terry towels produce. Try it with the thinnest glaze you can manage, if you're a brave sort, over a wall that has been painted a color you don't like. Applying it over vibrant color will produce an effect similar to a subtle haze over the wall. It's quite beautiful and worth a try in nearly any corrective complementary glaze color **(figures 19 and 20)**.

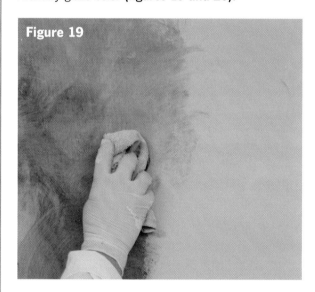
Figure 19

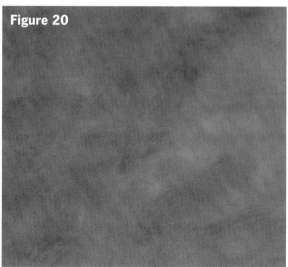
Figure 20

ragging off

Almost any type of rag will do—store-bought ones, an odd sock, old pajamas, or a T-shirt that has seen better days. Before you begin, prepare the rag by saturating it in water, and then wring it out thoroughly. Keep in mind that different types of rags will leave different impressions or patterns, depending mostly on the type of fabric and somewhat on how you bunch it up in your hand. Highly absorbent fabrics, such as cotton, will remove more glaze. Also, the same or similar fabrics will act differently upon a glaze, depending on how many times you have put the rags into the washing machine. For a consistent result, especially on a large surface, professional decorative painters always use store-bought rags **(figures 21 and 22)**.

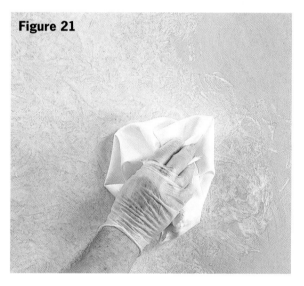
Figure 21

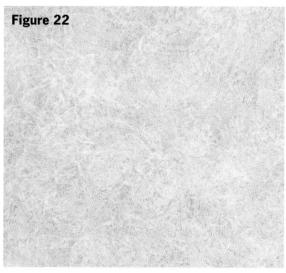
Figure 22

chamois glaze

Unlike a rag, a chamois, which is a type of soft leather, leaves a flower-like imprint in an oil glaze. It's a pretty finish that is considerably more subtle than that of a conventional sponge or rag technique. It's easier to render beautifully than a cheesecloth glaze, and you can successfully substitute an imitation (cotton) chamois for the real thing **(figures 23 and 24).**

Figure 23

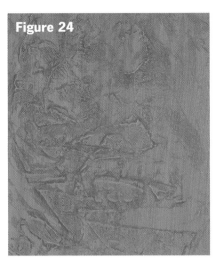

Figure 24

cheesecloth glaze

Other than a stippling brush, which I despise so much I am not even including its use for your consideration, cheesecloth will leave the finest, most subtle imprint in a glaze. Don't be fooled by this, however; imperceptible glaze-removal methods are tricky. First, you must apply the glaze evenly before removing it the same way—evenly. Second, it takes practice to get a feel for exactly how much glaze to remove from the wall. Working with a well-rinsed, unbleached cheesecloth is old-fashioned oil glazing at its finest and well worth the practice and patience to perfect it. Bunch a great big piece of cheesecloth together to make a soft ball. Apply the glaze evenly to the surface, and then just as evenly, pounce the glaze, removing a small and consistent amount as you move over the surface. As the cheesecloth gets soaked, it will remove less glaze. Transition to a clean cloth a little at a time in an attempt to create the appearance of working with the same cloth at the same saturation point from start to finish **(figures 25 and 26).**

Figure 25

Figure 26

more colors, more depth

In the end, the only limit to your imagination and choice of tool will not be your time and stamina, but it may be how many walls you can find to glaze! After over 20 years of glazing, and without a minute to spare, I kept playing in the glaze for quite a while after rendering these sample boards. Note that layering and working in two **(figure 27)** or three colors **(figures 28 and 29)** adds depth to the glazing.

Figure 27

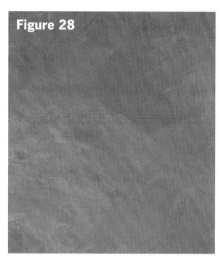

Figure 28

Figure 29

SUBTLE SHIFTS IN COLOR add interest to this wall. The trick to its understated look is in sensing how much of the glaze to remove.

A SENSATIONAL VENETIAN PLASTER FINISH—tinted red here—has been admired and desired for centuries because, without a doubt, it is a classic look that adds an unrivaled richness to any interior.

Venetian Plaster

The divine finish known as Venetian plaster, stucco lusto, and stucco Venetiano is as sought after today as it has been throughout history. But Venetian plaster is not a glaze, nor is it technically a textured finish. It is not even paint, and it is definitely not new. I suppose it could be considered earth-friendly, and while it does leave some pattern, well, that's not quite what Venetian plaster is all about, either. I have included it in this chapter because the technique is, by every definition, the quintessential classic; it really is the definitive finish of finishes.

Since Roman times, Venetian-plaster finishes have graced the most architecturally significant structures known to the ancient and modern world. Made of a combination of ground marble dust, wax, and dry pigments, today's basic mixtures can be found at your local home-improvement store. Whatever you can't find there is available from online sources.

be a pro

A SOUND FOUNDATION

The plaster will entirely conceal the underlying color, but not the wall's imperfections. The plaster and the blade will hang up on high spots, poorly patched areas, holes, dings, and so forth, so be sure to get the walls in very sound condition. A wall painted in a mid-sheen or eggshell base provides the perfect amount of "tooth" (grip) for the plaster.

design consult

BEFORE YOU PLASTER…Here are a few tips that will ensure a professional finish.

- If you are using new blades, file the sharp corners of the edges with 80-grit sandpaper. The rounded edges will leave fewer discernable lines in the plaster.
- Mix the plaster well to incorporate the color. The plaster will dry nearly two shades lighter than it appears in the can.
- Keep everything scrupulously clean as you are working—the plaster will dry quickly on the blade, in the mud pan, and on the wall. Make every effort to keep mixing the plaster to keep it wet. Pick little dry deposits out of the wall and off the blade. Clean the blade now and then with soapy water.

Venetian Plaster

paint saves the day

A lot of people complain that their plain walls look boring or lack architectural presence.

This is often a problem in new homes, especially when there is no trim-work or outstanding architectural feature. Venetian plaster is a creative way to add texture, patina, and character while expressing your artistry.

in the paint aisle

- Venetian plaster
- Venetian plastering blades
- 80-grit sandpaper
- Clean bucket
- Mud pan
- Large mixing stick or metal stirring hook for plaster
- Universal tint as needed

PLUS

- A bucket of soapy water

1 **Take up a small amount** of plaster evenly distributed on the blade, and start putting on the wall. Reload the blade with additional plaster as necessary.

2 **Work in a consistent, uniform fashion,** knowing that each stroke of the blade on the wall will be revealed in the final result. Choose a motion for the application with which you are comfortable, and stay with it throughout the entire application.

3 **I've applied the plaster** in a consistent horizontal, slightly downward line across the wall surface, and then crossed over it to remove excess plaster. Each mark of the blade appears as the darker line in the result.

4 **The plaster will begin to take up a shine** under the blade as each successive layer is applied. For a high sheen, apply a minimum of four coats of plaster. Rub the blade edge over the dry plaster in a scrubbing motion, and watch the shine begin to appear; again, find a position for your hand that feels comfortable to you, and then polish, polish, and polish again!

5 **It's optional,** but you can add a fine layer of clear paste wax. However, once you see the finished plaster, which will be beautiful and luminous, you may not dare do another thing to it.

the New
exciting products make

Fantastics

painting anything possible!

You've got an array of **innovative paints, additives, and related products** at your disposal today. Thanks to **these "new fantastics,"** you can render many of the types of finishes and transformations that **only professionals could do** in the past. What's also nice about these products and techniques is that, thanks to **quick-drying and specialty paints and finishes,** you can complete projects in a lot less time than in the past. In this chapter, you'll see how **creative ideas** and finishes take a kitchen from dilapidated to **delightfully charming.** What's more, you can easily find everything you need to **do it yourself** at your local home-improvement store.

ALL THIS KITCHEN NEEDED was a paint lift to give it style and charm. A rustic-grain finish brought together mismatched cabinets, and a faux stone completely changed the look of the plastic-laminate countertop. For pizzazz, I painted inexpensive tile for the backsplash.

the projects

Everyone knows a kitchen redo costs big bucks. But when a friend asked what I could do for next to nothing to improve a half-baked kitchen in their guest cottage, I said, "Paint it, of course!" Thanks to some nifty new paint products, I was able to give almost every surface more than a little makeover. Even the painted countertop holds up to wear!

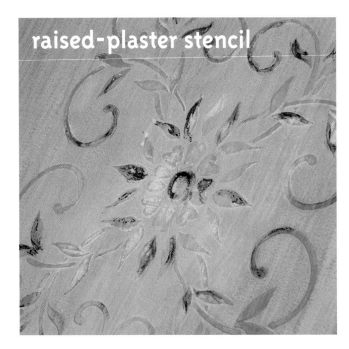

raised-plaster stencil

faux soapstone countertop

copper-painted tiles

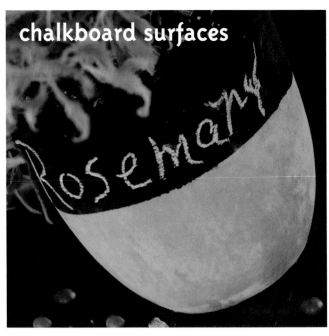

chalkboard surfaces

THIS CHARMING COTTAGE KITCHEN was a hodgepodge of mix-and-match cabinets and surfaces until paint and a few clever techniques rescued it.

Raised-Plaster Stencil on a Cottage Vinegar-Grained Finish

paint saves the day

A raised-plaster stencil on a cottage vinegar-grained finish comes to the rescue.

Removing the kitchen's built-in-place wall cabinets would have posed a new set of problems, so I had to find a way to "marry" them with the inexpensive, but much-needed, new base units. The stain does the trick and the stencil adds interest.

in the paint aisle

- Shellac-based primer
- Yellow milk paint
- A precut plaster stencil
- Joint compound or plaster
- Spackle blade
- White glue
- Tape
- India ink
- Universal tint in burnt umber
- Clear shellac
- Denatured alcohol
- Assorted brushes, buckets, mixing containers, stir sticks
- Satin-finish polyurethane (optional)

PLUS

- Cider vinegar, sugar, plastic cups

design consult

IT WOULD BE NEARLY IMPOSSIBLE to get the 80-plus-year-old cabinets smooth, and the possibility of old lead paint made sanding unwise. Because a fine finish was out of the question, a more naively executed, two-part wood-graining technique settled in nicely over the dense, dead-flat, and toothy milk paint. The vinegar technique is fun and uncomplicated, and a nod to the craftsmen of the day.

stencil the cabinet door fronts

1 **Wash and sand the cabinets**. Then apply the shellac-based primer. Next, paint the base coat. I chose an environmentally friendly milk paint in a soft, sunny yellow. Let it dry.

2 **Center the specialty stencil** on the face of each flat-panel door, and secure it with tape.

3 **Add a small amount of white glue** to the joint compound, and mix. This will help to prevent cracks and encourage adhesion. Apply the mixture with a blade, beginning at the top. Pull the blade down steadily to leave a somewhat even layer at the bottom.

4 **Remove the stencil** after a minute or two, and let the plaster dry overnight.

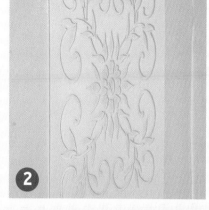

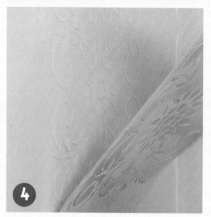

stain and "grain" the cabinets

5 **Mix together** a blob of burnt umber universal tint, 3 drops of India ink, ⅓ cup of cider vinegar, and 2 teaspoons of sugar in a plastic cup. Use it with a fan brush to simulate a wood grain.

6 **Next, make the vinegar "stain,"** or overglaze, by mixing a blob of burnt umber universal tint with 3 drops of India ink, ⅓ cup of cider vinegar, and 2 teaspoons of sugar. Stir it well. Use a small chip brush to apply the overglaze to the cabinets.

While the overglaze is still wet, soften the overall effect using a large, dry brush. You can create additional graining by dragging the brush through the overglaze.

7 **Emphasize details** in the raised plaster using a fine-art brush and both of the glaze mixtures. Then finish the doors with with three coats of clear, dead-flat varnish.

Faux Vermont Soapstone Countertop

paint saves the day

A painted faux Vermont soapstone update gives a plastic-laminate countertop new style.

If a stone countertop isn't in your budget, there are paint-like products that claim to simulate it. But I found rendering a faux stone with traditional paints to be easier. What's more, I've tested it, and the finish stands up remarkably well to everyday use and cleaning.

in the paint aisle

- Sander and assorted sandpapers
- Alcohol-based primer
- Universal tints in black and raw umber
- Flat-finish black latex paint
- Flat-finish off-white latex paint
- Denatured alcohol
- Sponges, putty, and a putty knife
- Satin-finish oil-based polyurethane (quick drying)
- Paste wax

PLUS

- White vinegar, a toothbrush, newspaper, and plastic wrap

prepare the surface for paint

1 Using an orbital sander and a 100-grit sandpaper, go over the existing laminate surface thoroughly and hard. Then wash it with a mixture of dish soap, white vinegar, and water. The vinegar will etch the surface and remove grease.

prime the surface

2 After it's dry, dust the surface, and then prime it with an alcohol-based high-adhesion primer.

3 Mix a black universal tint into the white primer to create a cold gray. (Make sure to mix enough paint to cover the entire surface.) Brush a heavy coat of the gray onto a small area on the countertop.

4 Immediately press a sheet of newspaper into the primer, smooth it into the wet paint **(4a),** and then remove it. The newspaper will leave a mottled and broken impression. Leave any highs and lows; do not be concerned if some areas do not look textured **(4b).**

5 While the primer is still tacky, pour a small amount of denatured alcohol into a plastic cup, and with a toothbrush, flick the alcohol over the primer here and there. If the primer begins to dry, place a piece of dry newspaper over the sprayed alcohol to help to "open" it. Don't get carried away, but continue over the entire length of the primed counter in a haphazard but natural-looking fashion. This will create small fossil-like holes in the primer.

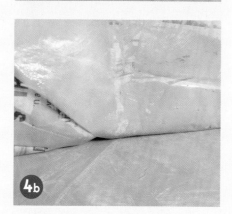

design consult

TOP-QUALITY PRIMERS AND MODERN PAINT FORMULATIONS make painting just about every surface possible. Here, shellac-based primer, which I worked into the technique, adds body and texture to the painted faux-stone countertop. I can report from experience that if your surface is clean and the bond is made good with a vinegar wash, the painted countertop will hold up surprisingly well to heavy kitchen use. If you treat the surface as you would genuine marble, cleaning spills quickly, using a cutting board, and keeping hot pots off the counter, you will gleefully arrive on the affirmative side of the "to paint or not to paint" debate.

apply the paint

6 **Fill two small separate containers** with the flat white paint, and fill a third with flat black paint. Add a little of the black paint to one of the containers with the white paint to tint it gray. Thin all three with water. Using a cellulose sponge, randomly dab the countertop with some white paint **(6a)**; do the same with a clean sponge and the black paint **(6b)**; and finally, add the gray in the same manner **(6c)**.

7 **While the paint is still wet,** press newspaper or plastic into the wet paint and smooth over it to create pattern and texture that resembles stone.

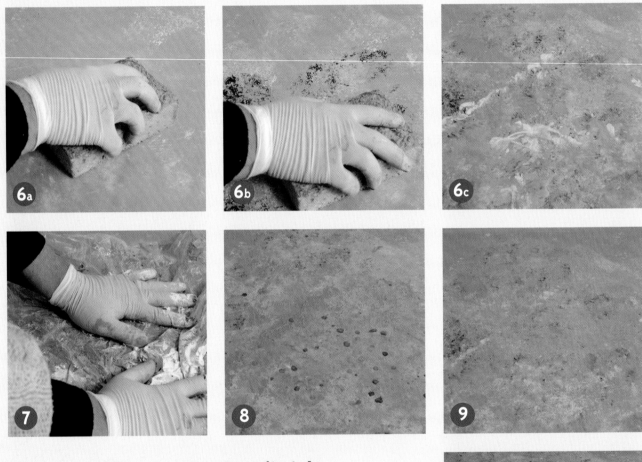

seal it with a protective finish

8 **Follow with a little** more flicking of the denatured alcohol to make some holes. Then flick on a little of the black paint.

9 **When it is dry,** the surface should look mottled.

10 **For the final finish,** use three coats of oil-based quick-dry polyurethane. Wet-sand between the second and third coat, and again when the final coat is dry, using a 400-grit wet/dry sandpaper. After a week, use a green scrubbing pad to apply a coat of paste wax, which you can tint to match the countertop.

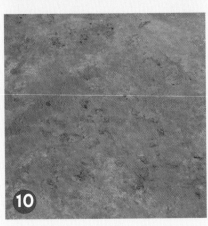

A STONE COUNTERTOP IS AN AMENITY that most homeowners want today. But if you must keep costs down, you can render the look of stone in paint. With proper care, a painted plastic-laminate surface will hold up until you can afford to replace it with the real thing.

Colorful "Copper" Tiles

paint saves the day

Turn inexpensive or mismatched ceramic tile into something fabulous.

I used two fantastic, readily available new products—metallic copper spray paint and glossy acrylic enamel craft paint. The latter is available in over 50 colors. (The manufacturer calls them "glossie" paints.) The product will adhere to nonporous glossy or glazed surfaces, and the colors are clear and bright. They dry with a delightful gleam that replicates the look of a fine imported tile. As a bonus, the paints intermix, cost under $4 for 2 ounces, and best of all, will hold up to a soap-and-water cleaning.

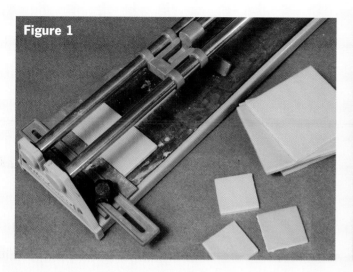

Figure 1

do the prep work

- **Wash the tiles** with distilled white vinegar and water. If the tiles are extremely dirty (old tiles, for example), wash them with hydrogen peroxide to remove all grease and grime from the surface.

- **If it's necessary to cut the tiles** to fit the installation, do it now. For example, I cut my bargain 4 x 4-inch tiles into smaller 2 x 2-inch pieces to suit the size of the backsplash and to add an upscale look to the design **(figure 1).**

- **If you are refinishing existing tile** in place, cover the grout lines with masking tape. Leave long tails on the tape so that it's easy to remove later. If the grout lines are too narrow to tape, cut a "paint window" out of a piece of acetate or paper and position it on each tile, securing it with the tape.

paint and decorate

- **Apply a base coat** to the tiles using a metallic copper spray paint in a glossy finish. Let the tiles dry, which they will do quickly.

- **Using the glossy craft paints,** apply one or an assortment of colorful abstract designs on each tile freehand.

design consult

YOU DON'T NEED TO BE A FINE ARTIST TO GET SMASHING RESULTS. Get the design started with rubber stamps, and finish it in your own signature colors. If you are stuck for an idea, buy a few of your favorite imported tiles, and use the motifs to inspire your own masterful creations. Some of the most beautiful Portuguese and Spanish tile designs are primitive. Graphic fine-china patterns are also a great source for inspiration.

DRESS UP A PLAIN BACKSPLASH with inexpensive standard tiles treated with an easy custom design. I painted these while I watched TV and it was actually relaxing!

Painted Chalkboard and Magnetic Niches

paint saves the day

You can use a nifty new additive to make any wall surface magnetic. Paired with matching chalkboard paint and framed, it's a swell display.

This is a handy idea for recipes, take-out menus, and notes. A fantastic product, the magnetic additive can be added to any latex primer. Then apply two coats of latex paint and, wonder of wonders, things will stick to it once it dries! Chalkboard paint that is not black adds another new twist. Follow the instructions exactly. Just use a contrasting chalk color to write. I made a simple frame out of scrap pine and ebonized it. (See "Ever So Faux," page 84.) You can use any stock frame for your project.

A WASH with bleach and water will prepare a terra-cotta pot for paint. The dampness of the plantings does not disturb the painted surface, and any mishaps when watering can easily be rewritten.

create the magnetic surface

- **Mask the areas** to be painted. Mix the magnetic additive into a latex primer. (See the manufacturer's instructions.) You'll need one bottle for about 400 square feet. Apply two coats of the primer followed by any-color latex paint **(figure 1)**.

create the chalkboard

- **Sand the area**. Mix 4 teaspoons of a pale sand-less grout and 1 cup of latex paint. Stir it well, and apply it using a disposable roller **(figure 2)**. Once it dries, run the side of a piece of chalk over the surface to condition it. Wipe off using a rag.

finish with the frame

- **Wait for the paint to dry,** then remove the tape. Install your frame.

in the paint aisle

FOR THE MAGNETIC WALL

- **Magnetic paint additive**
- **Latex primer**
- **Latex paint (any color)**
- **Masking tape**
- **Two small disposable short-nap rollers**

FOR THE CHALKBOARD

- **Sandless grout**
- **Flat latex paint**
- **A disposable short-nap roller**
- **Masking tape**
- **A piece of chalk (any color)**
- **A frame**

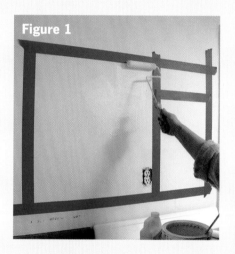

Figure 1

Figure 2

be a pro

MAGNETIC PERSONALITY

Yes, this is a fun way to hang notes and photos. You can even tack a recipe on the wall near the range or takeout menus near the phone. Just make sure to use strong magnets or stick up lightweight items only. Before you get started, bring the can to the paint department and ask someone to put it in the electric shaker. Otherwise, you'll have to stir it for at least 10 minutes. (Is your arm already getting numb?)

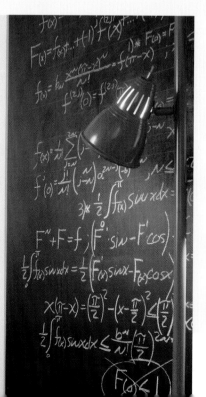

A BUSY MATH MAJOR has some fun with a sliding flat-panel door. This is a nice idea for the pantry or a basement stairwell, or to keep notes and records handy in a utility area.

CHAPTER 3

Yes, You Can

restore, repurpose, and save

Paint That

money by painting items that you already own

You may be astonished by the types of things around your house that you can rescue with paint—upholstery, curtains, lampshades, chandeliers, vinyl flooring, windows, and plastic-laminate cabinets to name a few. Yes, it's unconventional to paint an upholstered chair, for example, but it's doable—and with excellent results. Of course, you should weigh every paint decision against two factors: how much work is involved and the staying power of the result. But if an ugly or dated object or surface is interfering with your design goal, sometimes a little risk may be worth the gamble. In this chapter, see what paint can do for things you might otherwise toss or replace.

YES, I DID PAINT THIS WING CHAIR! The frame was sound, the fabric was intact—but soiled—and I saved oodles by painting rather than reupholstering the piece.

the projects

Now I'm not going to suggest that a painted rescue is always a dream solution, but when the budget is tight and you need to make a change, a beautifully rendered "paint lift" can be a great idea. Originality and artistic flair lend more than a little panache to such endeavors, especially when you pair these qualities with the right paints and know-how.

upholstery

chandelier

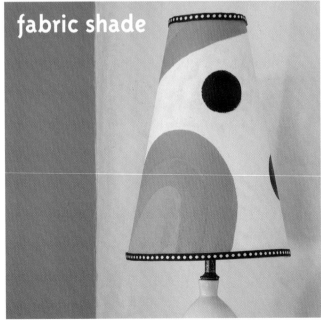

fabric shade

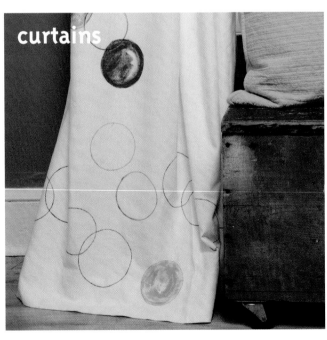

curtains

Use these projects as inspiration. Expand on them. I painted one plastic-laminate cabinet, but you can use my instructions and transform an entire kitchen. I added a little color to plain linen curtains, but you can paint flowers, stripes, butterflies, or any other motif onto pillows, table linens, duvet covers—virtually any fabric item in the house. Think big!

resilient vinyl

glass

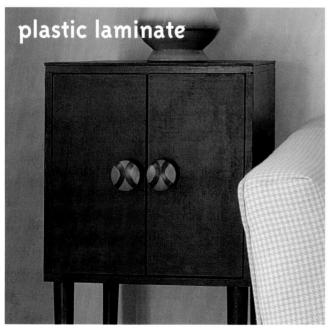

plastic laminate

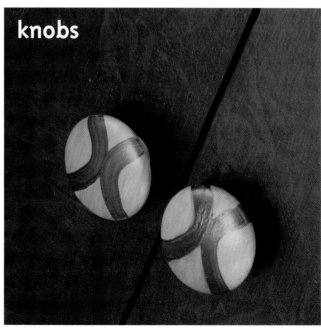

knobs

Paint Upholstery? Yes, You Can!

paint saves the day

Give dull or soiled upholstery a fresh, new look with paint and color.

A fabric-inspired painted design masks soiled areas and saves this chair for more lazy afternoon lounging. Paint your design freehand or use a stencil. Pick up a pattern or color from another element in the room.

in the paint aisle

- Colored pencil for fabric transfer
- Acrylic fabric paints in assorted colors, including white
- A palette for mixing
- Fine-art brushes

PLUS

- A stencil or acetate
- A craft knife
- An iron

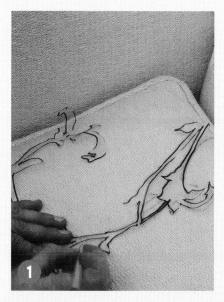

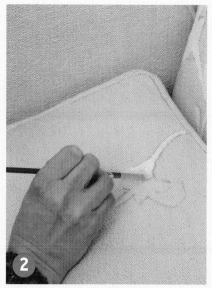

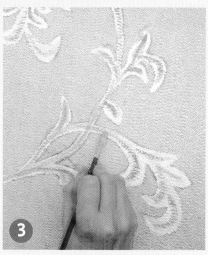

stencil & paint

1 **Position the stencil,** and secure it with pins. Trace the design onto the fabric using a colored pencil. (You can also use chalk, but the slubbed chenille fabric here would have made the tracing sloppy.)

2 **Use an artist's brush** and white soft-fabric paint as a "primer," filling in the areas outlined by the traced design. Let it dry.

3 **Color in your design** with acrylic fabric paint using a clean artist's brush. I started with golden yellow and worked my way through the design.

4 **Follow with additional colors** if your motif calls for them. Once the paint dries, erase the pencil marks, and set the pattern with a slightly warm iron. A coat of fabric sealer is optional; it will look a bit amber over white cloth.

design consult

THE CHARMING LEAFY DESIGN on the chair was easy to do using a homemade stencil and acrylic fabric paints. I borrowed a motif from a favorite piece of fabric, but you can use anything. Remember, you can enlarge or shrink your design on a copier machine. Then trace it onto stencil acetate, and cut it out using a craft knife. The painted surface will wear well, and you can customize the colors to suit the upholstered piece and the room.

From Shabby to Fabulously Chic Chandelier

paint saves the day

A light fixture can date a room, even if it's only the finish that's out of fashion.

All it takes is an afternoon and a high-performance oil-based enamel paint to give it an updated satin-nickel look.

Just make sure that the area where you are working is well ventilated. This paint gives off strong fumes.

clean and prep the fixture

- **Whether your chandelier is a recent garage-sale find** or the one that has been hanging over your table for the past 20 years, prepare it for paint by cleaning it. Use a toothbrush for extra-grimy areas.

- **If it's an existing fixture,** disconnect it and take it down. (Always cut the power at the circuit breaker before removing and when reinstalling a light fixture.) Mask the lightbulb receptacles with tape.

apply the paint

- **With the chandelier, including the chain, suspended from a ladder,** spray it entirely with blue high-performance oil-based enamel paint. You can touch up small pieces or nooks using a brush and paint from the ½-pint can.

- **Stir the clear varnish well,** and then tint it with a teaspoon of oil-based white paint. In another container, mix a dash of water with the gray paint; in a third container, add another dash of water to the metallic silver paint.

- **Pick up some of the gray** with a piece of moist but well-wrung cellulose sponge, and randomly apply the color over the blue base coat. Next, apply the varnish, dabbing it onto the fixture in a quick, pecking fashion over the blue and into the gray areas. Then, with a clean piece of the moist sponge, go back over the fixture one more time with the metallic silver paint.

- **The unconventional mixing** of oil- and water-based media will create highs and lows as the solvents fight each other. So with a dry artist's brush, fill in any voids using the metallic silver paint.

add a fine finish

- **Let the fixture dry overnight.** Then use a soft brush to whisk thinned black acrylic paint over the piece to settle things. Next, apply a light coat of shoe polish; pounce it on and buff it with a soft rag. Finish with a clear paste waxing.

in the paint aisle

- Blue high-performance, oil-based spray enamel in a semigloss finish or ½ pint of blue high-performance oil-based enamel
- 1 cup white oil-based paint
- Gray acrylic craft paint
- Silver-metallic acrylic craft paint
- Clear oil-based varnish
- Artist's brushes

PLUS
- A cellulose sponge cut into pieces
- A small tin of black shoe polish
- Clear paste wax
- A ladder

design consult

POLISHED NICKEL will appear more mottled and authentic when rendered in layers. Before you start, don't forget to mask the work area and make sure it's well ventilated. For surfaces too detailed to brush, substitute blue high-performance spray enamel. If the metal will get wet or is in any way exposed to moisture, apply marine vanish before you add the shoe-polish coating.

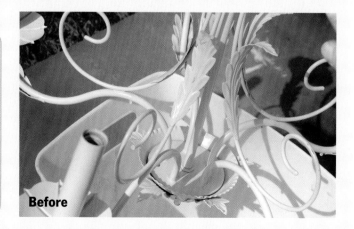

Before

A Groovy Look for Lampshades

paint saves the day

Funky flea-market finds, these lamps needed a shade makeover. No problem!

A fabric-inspired modern graphic and a little paint will make the old pair a trendy triumph. No worries about painting over stains; a spray of shellac provides a good base for paint. The important thing to remember is to apply the paint evenly; the design will be backlit by the bulbs, which will reveal any patchy spots. For a finish with a flourish, I glued fabric trimming to the top and bottom edges.

design consult

IF YOU WANT THE SHADE TO HAVE REFLECTIVE VALUE, use silver- or gold-toned spray paint on the inside surface. For more transparent looks on linen, experiment with watercolors or thinned acrylic paints. Paper shades can take a high-gloss treatment well. You can execute it in elaborate cutout patterns that you can mask with tape or clear adhesive vinyl. (Stick with a low-watt bulb for safety's sake.)

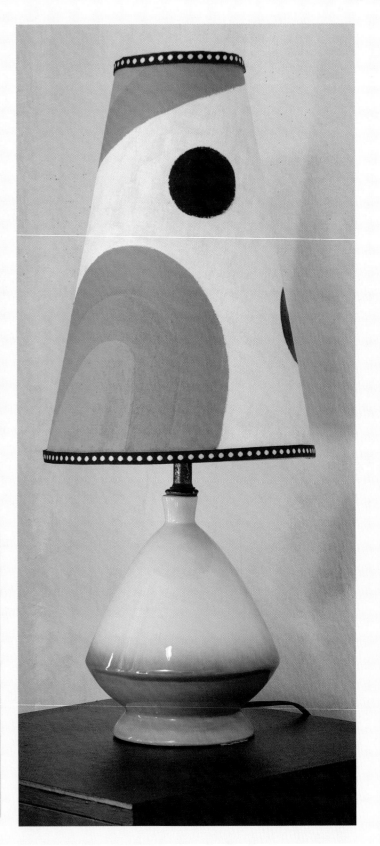

prepare the shades for painting

1 Spray the inside and outside of the shade with two coats of clear shellac, which acts as a bonding agent, barrier coat, and primer. In this case, it also levels the slubbed texture of the linen weave.

apply the design and paint

2 Use graphite transfer paper to render a fabric-inspired design. Tape the graphite transfer paper onto the surface of the shade; then position your design on top of it. Use a pencil to lightly trace the outline of the design onto the shade. Use a fine-art brush, and begin painting, starting with the palest color. Use a clean brush for each color. Don't recoat any mistakes, but rather, work each stroke of the brush into the final design. For fine lines, use paint pens.

3 For the finish, apply two coats of crystal-clear, matte–finish spray varnish. Then glue fabric trim or ribbon to the edge of the painted shade. Voilà!

Yes, You Can Paint Washable Textiles

paint saves the day

Give plain curtains, coverlets, and pillows a paint lift. It's easy!

Why settle for boring when the simplest painted design can add a hip vibe? If you have a patterned carpet, such as an Oriental, try to reproduce one of its motifs. Fabric paint is available in a full range of washable, spirited colors.

in the paint aisle

- Soft white or black* fabric paint
- Acrylic textile medium
- Fabric paint in assorted colors
- Fine-art brushes

design consult

SHOP HARD FOR A BARGAIN, knowing that you can transform the most mundane textiles into compelling decorative accents with paint. Machine-washable cotton, muslin, denim, and linen all take fabric paint quite nicely. Don't overlook what you may already have stashed in the back of the closet, either; well-loved vintage table linens that are stained can be made new again with novel painted designs. For starters, keep it simple, maybe with an understated monogram, or use a stencil if you're a little shaky with a brush.

ready the fabric and map your design

1 **Before you do anything,** wash the fabric in regular detergent without additives of any kind, and choose a long or extra-rinse cycle to be sure no softener residue can resist the paint.

Using a light pencil, sketch, trace, or lay out your design on the fabric. I painted simple, overlapping circles using a ceramic lid to trace them.

apply the paint

2 **Prime the circles.** Mix a little textile medium with the white fabric paint, and apply one coat. (*Use black fabric paint for dark designs.)

3 **While the primer is still wet,** finish the design in color using fabric paints that have also been thinned with textile medium. Avoid heavy layers of paint, which will crack and melt a little when the piece goes in the dryer after a washing.

be a pro

PERFECT PAINTING
Always iron out wrinkles or creases in any fabric before you apply your design or paint. If you're painting a large piece of fabric, such as a curtain panel, you can lay it flat on a clean surface, such as a tabletop. But make sure to protect the surface from bleeding paint by sandwiching plastic sheeting between it and the fabric.

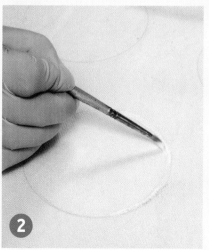

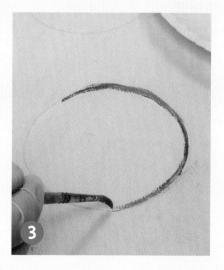

Paint Resilient Vinyl? No Kidding!

paint saves the day

High-performance enamel comes to the rescue of a dull, imitation-wood-pattern resilient-vinyl floor.

How well this paint job will hold up has more to do with the quality of the flooring material than the paint. Heavy grades of resilient-vinyl sheet flooring and good old linoleum are very accepting of paint.

be a pro

IF YOU HAVE A FLOOR THAT'S IN IFFY SHAPE, cover it with the least-expensive sheet vinyl you can find, but install it upside down. The underside accepts paint like a charm. It's a nice trick for great floor cloths and ad hoc area rugs, too.

DO NOT THIN THE VARNISH. If necessary, you can add a few drops of Japan dryer to speed things up a little. However, don't work out of the varnish can unless you plan to use it all because the dryer will not store well in the product.

in the paint aisle

- Trisodium phosphate (TSP)
- 80-grit sandpaper
- 3-pound cut shellac
- Denatured alcohol
- High-adhesion alcohol-based primer
- High-performance oil-based enamel or artist's oils
- Universal tints
- Lamb's wool applicator or natural-bristle brush
- Short-nap roller
- Marine varnish
- Japan dryer (optional)

PLUS

- Towels

prepare the surface

1 **Wash the floor well with** trisodium phosphate (TSP). Rough up the surface a bit with an 80-grit sandpaper; vacuum; and dust. Map out a simple design. In this case, I used masking tape to create large triangles. (See Chapter 6, "Pattern...Panache for Pennies," for information about taping.)

2 **Thin the shellac** by 25 percent, and then brush it over the areas to be painted using a clean, natural-bristle brush. The thinned shellac will dry fast.

prime and paint the floor

3 **Coat the floor** with the primer using a short-nap roller. It will dry fast, and you can apply a second coat for added durability. Then apply two coats of high-performance enamel. You can add any color to the paint using a universal tint. (If you are doing a faux, glazed, or patterned design over the base coat, you can skip the second coat.) Let the base coat dry. Use a bold-color high-performance oil-based paint for the triangles. For more detailed designs, you can use artist's oils. (See Chapter 8, "Painted Floors.") Use a lamb's wool applicator or a natural-bristle brush to apply marine varnish over the painted areas. This will protect the paint from foot-traffic wear.

Keep in mind that varnish is slow to dry—even more so when it's applied to vinyl. It also draws dust like crazy. Place well-wrung wet towels in the doorways to keep the dust in adjoining rooms from floating into the finish.

4 **Remove the masking tape** carefully. Pull it toward the paint, rather than away from it. Make sure the floor is completely dry before walking on it or replacing furniture.

Fantabulous Frosted Glass

paint saves the day

You don't have to sacrifice privacy or light when a window is awkardly located.

Here, semitransparent frosted-glass stripes are deceptively simple to paint and add architectural rhythm to the curious interior window that allows light and air into a diminutive second-floor landing.

design consult

FROSTING PAINT is the dark horse of the paint world. The list of possible applications is long, and I dare say obscuring an undesirable view, creating privacy, reinventing globe light fixtures, personalizing glass-cabinet doors, and introducing color and architectural pattern to clear glass are merely the most obvious ones. What's more, it's an easy and inexpensive project that has the look and feel of etched glass. But you must apply it to a squeaky-clean surface. Use a commercial glass cleaner, or check your local hardware store for the tiny red box of dry powder that professional window washers use. Add a little vinegar and water to it, and you'll have the professional formula for making all of your windows and glass doors sparkle like crazy!

prepare the area

1 Mask the area around the glass—the sash, the sill, and the casing. I removed the window, making it easier to rinse. Be sure to prepare the area well for the rinsing if you are leaving the sashes in place.

Clean the glass thoroughly, and dry it well. Also, be sure the surface is not cold before applying the coating.

I used masking tape, burnishing the edges well, to create my simple stripes. However, self-adhesive window film is better for creating elaborate designs.

apply the coating

2 Wearing rubber gloves, coat the surface with the etching medium.

3 Let the finish stand for at least 30 minutes. (Check the label on the etching medium for the manufacturer's recommendation.) Wash the medium off the glass, using a sponge, lots of rags, and clean water. Then remove the tape.

Apply a drop of lighter fluid to a small cotton swab, which you can use to clean off any residue of the etching medium that may have leeched under the tape. If future cleaning will include a commercial product, protect the frosted glass by spraying on a clear, nonyellowing acrylic finish. Otherwise, use a mild vinegar-and-water solution for cleaning.

in the paint aisle

- Glass-etching medium
- Masking tape
- Clear, nonyellowing, acrylic spray finish
- Paintbrush

PLUS

- Window-washing detergent or rubbing alcohol
- Glass cleaner
- Vinegar (optional)
- Clean rags
- Rubber gloves
- Sponge
- Lighter fluid (optional)
- Cotton swab (optional)

be a pro

"ETCHING" EXPERTISE

Read the medium label carefully. Some manufacturers recommend treating the glass with a surface conditioner that is a bonding agent. Do not skip this step if it is recommended; the product is not expensive (about $3). For intricate designs, use a paintable masking fluid to isolate the work and protect the glass. If you choose the masking-fluid medium, first wash your brush with soap and water and dip it into brush cleaner. Then load it with the fluid. This will prevent the medium from quickly becoming gunky and ruining the brush forever. It's hard to sacrifice a good brush, but the cheapies may not give you the accuracy you need.

Perfectly Paintable Plastic Laminate

paint saves the day

Paint plastic-laminate cabinets and furniture? You betcha!

A lot of creative spirit transforms a plain plastic-laminate box into a chic faux-leather cabinet. If you're doing a standard paint job—on plastic-laminate kitchen cabinets, for example—make sure to clean and degrease them thoroughly, and then apply an oil-based primer. Also, wear gloves and a respirator (and it's probably a good idea to shut off the stove's pilot light) because the fumes are strong.

in the paint aisle

- American vermillion Japan paint
- 80- and 220-grit aluminum oxide sandpaper
- Tack cloths
- Universal tints in burnt umber and burnt sienna
- Mineral spirits
- Oil-based glaze
- Paint thinner
- Japan dryer or oil-based paint in a dark color
- Chamois
- Buckets, stir stick, and brushes

PLUS

- Vinegar
- Water
- Rubber or latex gloves
- A respirator

prepare the surface and apply a base coat

1 Sand the laminate hard, using the 80-grit sandpaper. Then wash it with a mixture that is equal parts vinegar and water; dry it, and then go over the plastic laminate with a tack cloth.

Paint the entire surface with two coats of American Vermillion Japan paint or a vibrant red high-performance oil-based enamel.

Lightly sand the painted surface using 220-grit sandpaper; go over it with a clean tack cloth.

add the tinted-glaze layer and finish

2 Mix a heavy red and dark-brown oil glaze made up of 4 parts glaze, 1 part mineral spirits, and universal tints in burnt umber and burnt sienna. The tinted glaze should be a deep color. Add Japan dryer or a little black or dark brown oil-based paint to ensure that the mixture will dry.

Brush on the glaze. While it's still wet, mottle it using a soaked but well-wrung chamois to simulate a leather appearance.

Crumple the chamois into the shape of a rosebud, and press it into the glaze to create the pattern **(2a).** On larger surfaces, roll the chamois up and down the glaze for even coverage **(2b).**

3 Finish the piece using new hardware. Here, I used a dash of acrylic paint for an artsy design that turns simple wood knobs, which cost less than $1 each, into one-of-a-kind pieces. A top coat of clear acrylic spray varnish protects their finish against daily wear.

design consult

MANY LARGE RETAILERS sell affordable furniture pieces made of fiberboard and factory-finished in a plastic laminate suggesting a wood grain or in plain white or black. Useful? Yes. Beautiful? Not so much. Oil-based Japan paints and high-performance oil-based enamels can banish the uglies and transform them into gems. The finishes can do the same for plastic-laminate cabinets, too.

be a pro

SHOE POLISH FINESSE

Experienced decorative painters rarely miss a chance to exploit the value of shoe polish. Similar to tinted paste waxes, shoe polish can be buffed to a beautiful shine when a little water is sprinkled over the surface. It's cheap and available in a few good colors, and it will take a tint. Shoe polish will add protection similar to that of wax and is especially useful for finishing metal. (See the chandelier on page 58.) Substitute a spray polyurethane if you think you'll repaint the piece in the future; shoe polish resists paint as surely as wax.

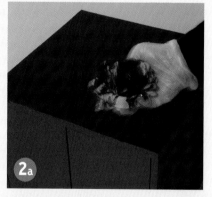

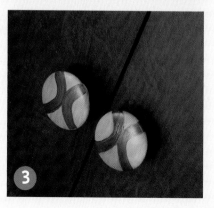

CHAPTER 4

Ever So...

paint and ingenuity

Faux!
add authentic touches

If you have a ho-hum area that lacks architectural interest, consider a faux finish—a **painted rendition** of a **natural material**. Conveying the formidable intensity associated with **stone** or the warmth of **wood** using a little paint is an enterprise that is worth pursuing. In this chapter, you'll find projects that show you techniques for **faux limestone** blocks and slabs, a **"marble"** tabletop, an **"ebony"** table, **rustic graining**, and **clair bois**, another wood-graining technique. In each case, the project rescued a tired or damaged surface. To make your faux treatment **believable**, take into account whether the real thing would be realistic in its place.

FAUX LIMESTONE BLOCKS, subtle yet handsome in their rendering, complete the look in this kitchen and dining area so perfectly that it's almost unimaginable to consider plain painted walls in their stead. The key to the technique's success is careful taping and the right application of paint.

the projects

The design community has a great appreciation for fantastical stone at the moment. While some techniques fall victim to trends in much the same way as skirt lengths, it is, nonetheless, a useful craft to render faux stone—in this case limestone and marble—in even the most simplified fashion.

faux limestone blocks

ebonizing

faux limestone slabs

And while there are tools and methods with which faux-bois techniques can be authentically rendered, sometimes the mere suggestion of wood is all that's needed to save a surface. Considered naive by expert faux finishers, this more subtle method can be useful on surfaces that would not suffer from a lack of intricately layered graining.

rustic graining

faux marble

clair bois

Faux Limestone Blocks

paint saves the day

When you've redone your kitchen, bath, or entry with gorgeous stone floors or counters, finish the look with a handsome faux treatment for the walls.

You can paint the "mortared stone"directly over existing beige paint. But if the surface is any other color, apply a good alcohol-based primer and two coats of a medium beige latex paint, which will be your "grout" color. A common block measures 8 x 16 inches. Still true to these proportions, larger 9 x 18-inch blocks are a better fit for this wall. When you're painting, treat each block as its own entity. Render some with a sponge, some with paper, and others with a combination of tools. You don't have to apply the colors in any special proportion or order. That way, the blocks will have an understated, random—and natural, of course—quality to them.

in the paint aisle

- Measuring tape, carpenter's square, level, and story pole
- Alcohol-based primer
- Flat latex paint in gray, medium beige, and two other closely related shades of beige
- Latex paint conditioner or water
- $1/8$-inch specialty masking tape
- Slanted-tip transparent art marker in sepia
- Assorted sponges, newspaper, and brushes

be a pro

CARPENTERS OFTEN USE A STORY POLE when one consistent measurement is repeated throughout a project. While I can't claim any credit for this nifty idea, I can report that it is a big help when laying out blocks, grids, stripes, or any repetitive measurement in a space. Even if you decide to do the measuring, the pole will happily warn you of mistakes and crooked tape and keep things moving along nicely if there is no one around to hold the other end of the measuring tape.

A story pole is easy to make. Cut a straight piece of wood to length. Use a carpenter's square and mark the consistent measurement all along the length of the pole. Then draw an easy-to-read straight line across it. Use a long level to make sure the line is plumb. You can now use your story pole to transfer the measurements directly onto the entire length and width of your wall.

design consult

FROM MODEST TO MAGNIFICENT, the success of faux-stone effects relies heavily on carefully planned color choices. Closely related shades of complex gray neutrals and earthy beiges in a balanced mix of cool and warm tones will produce the most authentic representations of stone. Add any single deviation, perhaps a darker gray as shown in the faux-limestone wall on the opposite page, and you'll have all the color necessary for a virtually foolproof and entirely convincing result.

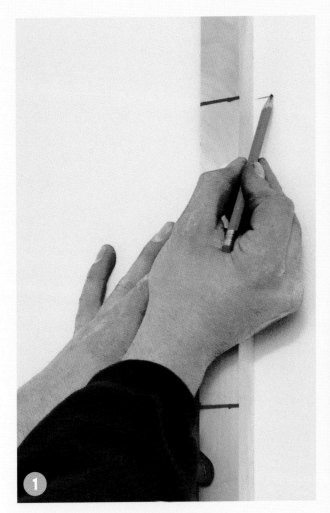

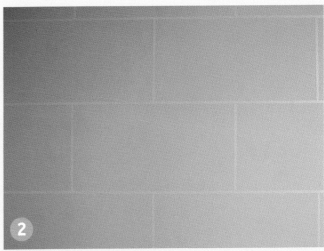

tape the blocks

1 **After you apply a new base coat**, let it dry completely. Note the measurements of your blocks in tiny pencil lines on the wall using a story pole as a guide. (See "Be a Pro" on the previous page.)

2 **Tape the horizontal "grout" lines**, using a ⅛-inch specialty masking tape, working from one end of the wall to the other. Leave a long tail on one end so you can pull off the tape later. Tape each vertical line, every 9 inches in this case, using one continuous piece of tape, intersecting the horizontal lines. Work from top to bottom.

Beginning at the top row on the left side of the wall, cut and remove every other vertical tape line to reveal the full-size block. Next, beginning again at the left side and skipping one block to create the stagger, once again remove every other vertical tape line. Repeat down the wall.

paint the blocks

3 **Thin each color** with a latex-paint conditioner or water. Pick up a little of one color using a natural sea sponge, and beginning in the middle of the block, dab the paint in a pecking, haphazard fashion. Pick up another color with a brush. Brush and pounce some of it inside the block. Then blend the colors subtly with a large, damp cellulose sponge; don't over blend.

4 **Move to another block.** For a more natural and less uniform look, skip around instead of working on consecutive blocks. This time, apply the paints with a different tool—in this case, newsprint. Press the newspaper over the paint, and smooth it out with your hand. Remove the paper to reveal the sandy-looking texture **(4a).** Add a little more interest with another color, using any of the sponges or a brush. Continue this approach, rendering each block a little differently **(4b).**

5 **The work will dry quickly,** after which you can remove the vertical tape. Pull it slowly toward itself. Then peel away all of the horizontal tape. A razor or dental pick is handy if the tape has set into the paint.

6 **Add optional shadow lines** when the blocks are thoroughly dry. Using a small fine-art brush and a straightedge of your choosing, add a shadow line to the inside left vertical "grout" edge and to the top of the lower horizontal "grout" edge of each block. Blur the lines with a damp rag. A natural shadow would be cast over the block from the light source, which can be implied in paint if there are no windows in the room.

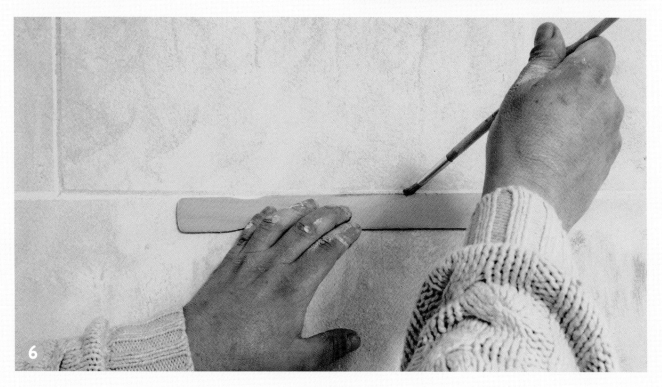

Mixed-Media Faux Limestone Slabs

paint saves the day

A stone-inspired finish can change a plain wall from bland to dramatic, which makes it a great idea for a room that needs a focal point or a stronger architectural presence.

I rendered a mixed-media effect in an unexpected modern green that is a faux version of three vertical limestone slabs. The finish went over an existing gray wall, but it would be equally effective over white, gray, or any pale-color surface. If you are repainting, prime and use a base coat.

in the paint aisle

- Measuring tape, measuring tools
- Alcohol-based primer
- Flat latex paint in brown, off-white, and beige
- ¼-inch specialty masking tape
- Oil-based glazing liquid
- Universal tints in Payne's Gray and light green
- Roller pan and roller
- Mineral spirits
- Buckets, sea sponge

mark and tape the wall

1 **If you are repainting,** first apply an alcohol primer to the wall and then two coats of gray or any pale-color paint.

   Once the base coat is completely dry, measure and mark oversize "limestone slabs," taping them vertically with a ¼-inch specialty masking tape. In this case, I created three equal-size slabs.

paint the "stone"

2 **Render the stone in two colors:** a well-thinned brown latex paint and a simple gray oil glaze composed of 4 parts oil-based glazing liquid and 1 part paint thinner that has been tinted with the Payne's Gray.

   Using a moist sea sponge (saturated in water and then wrung out well), apply the thinned brown latex paint to the wall in a random fashion. Without cleaning the sponge or allowing the paint to dry, load the sponge with the gray oil glaze. Apply the glaze directly into and over the brown paint.

   The incompatible latex and oil products will create a "resist," or a peeling reaction; allow this battle to ensue, and soften things with a dry brush whisked and pounced over the product combination. Note the amount of "age" and texture the mixed media creates.

3 **Continue to create the stone effect** while the oil glaze is still wet. Load a roller with a small amount of flat white latex paint, and roll it into the wet gray oil glaze in a soft and quick motion. Do not press on the roller, but skim over the top of the glaze and deposit an inconsistent amount of the white paint.

4 **Allow the paint and glaze to dry well,** and then apply a heavy green scumble glaze over it. The scumble glaze should consist of 4 parts oil-based glazing liquid and 4 parts mineral spirits, tinted with light green and cobalt universal tints. You can substitute the green-blue glaze with beige, white, gray, or a blue glaze, which are equally effective.

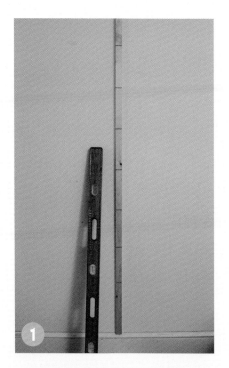

be a pro

YOU CAN SOFTEN any peeling using a dry brush. Do not overblend or correct too much; an overglaze can settle the final result. If you blend too much or want more complexity in the "stone," a wet rag can open the finish. Or go over it with a rag that is moistened with a small amount of paint thinner.

Faux Marble

paint saves the day

Fresh color and a new painted-marble top make this vintage piece of furniture better-looking than ever.

Japan paint, which you can tint, is more suitable for fine furniture because you can sand it; a satin alkyd or eggshell latex paint are acceptable alternatives, in that order, if you do not wish to mix your own color.

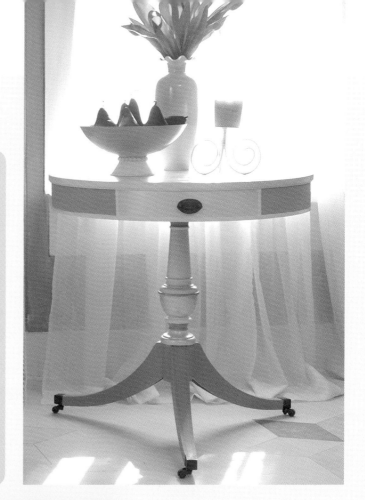

clean and prime the table

1 Remove any hardware, and then sand the entire table with 220-grit sandpaper. Clean the sanded table, washing it with a solution of water and vinegar. Let it dry, and then dust the table and wipe it with a tack cloth.

Once the table is clean, brush on an alcohol-based primer. Then go over the primed piece with 300-grit wet/dry sandpaper used dry.

Mix a pale blue-gray paint using the white Japan paint and the black, cobalt blue, and light-green universal tints; apply two coats.

Sand the painted wood surfaces with 300-grit wet/dry sandpaper used wet.

If the table has a leather top, cover it with two coats of white gesso. If the top is wood, apply two coats of an alcohol-based primer. Then wet-sand the surface well using 300-grit wet/dry sandpaper. Sanding with a lot of water creates a very smooth finish.

render the faux marble tabletop

2 Apply a tinted glaze (4 parts oil-based glazing liquid, 4 parts mineral spirits, and the dark raw umber). Squeeze some black, yellow ochre, and green acrylic paints onto a paper plate; thin each one with a little water. Apply a loose interpretation of black veining using an artists brush. *(continued on page 82)*

in the paint aisle

- Assorted sandpapers
- Alcohol-based primer
- White artist's gesso
- Japan paint in Flake White
- Universal tints in black, light green, raw umber, and cobalt blue
- Oil-based glazing liquid
- White oil-based paint
- Mineral spirits
- Tack cloth
- Acrylic paints in black, mint green, and yellow ochre
- Natural-bristle softening brush
- Assorted art brushes

PLUS

- Plastic sheeting

be a pro

KNOWING WHEN TO STOP can be the most challenging impediment to a really great faux marble. Most professional decorative artists will confess to having ruined a perfectly lovely marble effect with one last, unnecessary stroke of the brush. If this happens to you, the glaze and veining can be removed. Applying an additional glaze layer will usually remedy any mistakes. But remember, less is more.

(continued from page 81)

3 Immediately after painting the veins, go over them using a soft, natural-bristle brush or a badger-hair brush to blur them. Do this quickly, because the thinned acrylic will dry very fast.

4 Apply additional thinned yellow ochre and thinned green acrylic paint to the vein structure, and again, soften the appearance with a small fan brush and a natural-bristle brush.

5 Wait for the entire surface to dry, and then cover it with a basic gray glaze (4 parts alkyd glazing medium and 4 parts solvent, tinted with the white Japan paint and the black universal tint). Apply the glaze, and break it up using a crumpled piece of plastic; then soften it with a dry brush. This will not disturb the work done in acrylic paints.

Wait for the gray glaze to dry, and then apply a white scumble glaze, consisting of 6 parts glazing liquid, 1 part mineral spirits, and 1 part white oil paint.

Note: The scumble glaze will need a little thinning, or it will disturb the gray oil-glaze layer. (If you're worried about it, an isolating coat of thinned, clear shellac will prevent this from happening.)

After the white scumble glaze has dried, apply two coats of clear, nonyellowing latex polyurethane over the surface. Then wet-sand it with 600-grit wet/dry paper. Applying a final coat of clear, nonyellowing, paste wax will ensure this table's fine-furniture status.

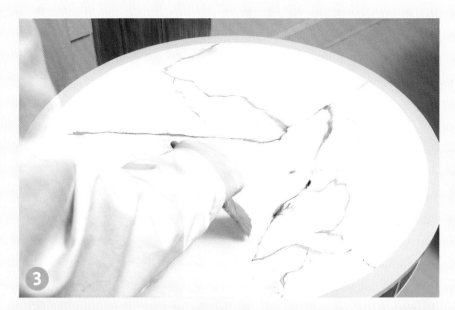

HERE IT IS—before I added color and a faux-marble finish to the top. This good-looking piece was sound and had graceful lines. All it needed was a paintlift.

be a pro

VEINS

Think of them as drifts of color that have a blurred appearance and flow in one direction. Avoid making the ends of the shapes into sharply painted triangles—keep them irregular. Vary the lines in width. Sharper veins can intermix with these drifts, but don't criss-cross them like an X or make them wiggly.

Ebonizing

paint saves the day

Maybe you've found an old wood chest, table, bookcase, or cabinet at an auction or antique fair that is still sturdy but could stand some updating.

If you love the modern look of today's espresso-toned, "ebonized" furniture, with proper preparation, and in one afternoon, you can turn any hodgepodge assortment of odd-ball pieces into a stylishly matching set. Real ebony is delicate and quite expensive, but you can make your piece hard-wearing with a latex polyurethane finish tinted with the same formula used to color the glaze. Apply two coats, which will add even more depth to the piece.

design consult

EBONIZED ESPRESSO

Sound vintage tag-sale finds, grandma's hand-me-downs, and painted doors and floors in especially bad condition are all good candidates for this easy, modern look. If you are not sure whether the piece has been waxed, test it. Take a sharp straight razor, lay it flat on the surface, and then pull it toward you in a few short strokes to see if there is a crumbly, yellow wax residue. If so, sand the furniture hard, clean it using paint thinner, and then retest. If you're still in doubt, apply a bonding agent for good measure and prime the piece with three coats of shellac-based primer.

clean and prime the piece

1 **Sand the wood,** using 200-grit sandpaper. Wash it with a vinegar and water solution; then dust it with a tack cloth. Apply an alcohol-based primer; then go over the piece again with 400-grit wet/dry sandpaper used wet.

Turn the piece upside down, and paint every part of the table that will be visible with a flat black latex. (Japan paint is better suited to melamine and fiberboard pieces; use artist's acrylic for smaller display pieces.) Turn the piece right side up, and apply the black paint. Apply additional coats as needed.

glaze and finish the piece

2 **Mix a simple oil glaze** made up of 4 parts oil-based glazing liquid and 1 part paint thinner. Make it dark brown, using equal parts of raw umber, burnt umber, and burnt sienna universal tints. Apply the glaze layer over the sanded black base coat using a good-quality brush. The heavy glaze will run like crazy, so keep an eye out for drips. Allow the piece to dry in a warm, clean place.

3 **Apply two coats** of cordovan paste shoe polish if you love the piece and do not think you will ever repaint it. Then dunk a green scrub pad into soapy water, and use it to polish the wax finish. Rub the wax in a circular motion; dry and buff the piece with a clean rag.

Forgo step 3 if the furniture has to stand up to hard wear. Instead, apply two coats of a protective polyurethane finish. Use the three universal tints to match the color of the glaze.

in the paint aisle

- Alcohol-based primer
- 200-grit sandpaper
- 400-grit wet/dry sandpaper
- Flat latex paint in black
- Oil-based glazing liquid
- Universal tints in burnt umber, burnt sienna, and raw umber
- Cordovan paste shoe polish
- Mineral spirits or paint thinner
- Tack cloth

Rustic Graining

paint saves the day

What's another way to restore beauty to old wood surfaces that must withstand a lot of wear and have been painted again and again?

In this case, I applied a rustic faux-bois paint technique to 200-year-old stair treads—and that saved the day! The glaze is a close representation of an old-fashioned asphaltum formula. There is a bit of thievery and trickery involved, however, because some of the ingredients in the original formula are not readily available today. This is a nice formula for rustic grains. Although I describe it as a specific recipe, rigid measuring is not necessary. The mixture stores well in a metal can and will come in handy for other faux-bois projects, easy furniture touch-ups, and other quick fixes.

be a pro

UNDERSTANDING WOOD
For a realistic rendering of wood, it's wise to study the type you wish to create in paint. Every wood species has its own grain pattern and color. In addition to straight grain, there's V-grain wood. Mahogany, for example, may come in either type of grain.

mix the oil-based formula

- **Set aside** about ¼ cup of the golden brown paint. Empty the remaining paint into a 2-gallon bucket.

- **Fill the empty can** a quarter of the way with mineral spirits. Spoon out approximately 8 tablespoons of the solids from the bottom of the wood stain can—don't shake or stir it. Mix this "goo" with the mineral spirits. Stir it well.

- **Add enough oil-based glazing liquid** to the new, gooey stain mixture to nearly fill the can. Stir this well, and then blend 8 teaspoons of black and 4 teaspoons of burnt umber into the mixture.

- **Pour this mixture** into the 2-gallon bucket containing the poured-off golden brown paint. Add the remaining glazing liquid.

  Stir the remaining stain from which you have stolen the tinting goo, and add half of it to the 2-gallon bucket. Stir the mixture well before using it.

  The graining concoction is a very heavy, densely tinted mixture. You can drag it and figure it with a brush to create a realistic pattern. You will have to add a fair amount of Japan drier to it in order to speed the drying time. Note: do not add the drier to the entire formula; limit it to what you will use for a day's work.

in the paint aisle

- 1 quart golden brown oil-based paint
- 1 quart oil-based, dark-color wood stain
- Mineral spirits
- Universal tints in black and burnt umber
- Japan drier

apply the grained finish

1 **Sand the surface** (in this case, stair treads, newel post, and railing) completely, using an 80-, 120-, and then 220-grit aluminum oxide sandpaper. Clean the surface thoroughly, and then apply an alcohol-based primer followed by two coats of a medium golden orange flat latex paint.

2 **Place a rolled up damp towel** at the top of the stairs. Unroll it as you complete each tread to keep dust from flying down into the wet stain. Starting with the top tread, dust and wipe with a tack cloth.

(continued on page 88)

(continued from page 87)

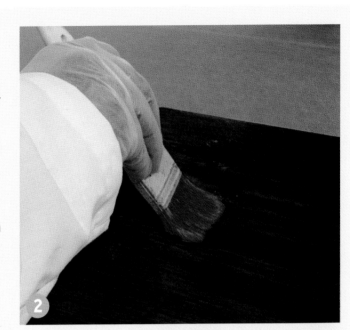

2 Apply the graining mixture to the tread, working from the left to the center, and then from the right to the center. Push a dry chip brush through the stain and flog. (Flogging is a rhythmic bouncing motion, which you make on and off the stain while you keep the brush moving across the surface. There are special flogging brushes for this, but they are too long for stair treads.)

3 Using the paint you set aside, add some thin lines with a small fine-art brush or a fan brush to suggest grain **(3a)**. You can drag the fan brush, torn cardboard, a notched comb, or steel wool through the wet glaze in order to add interest and to suggest a wood grain **(3b and 3c)**. (See "Be a pro," on page 86.)

Keep the work area, particularly the painted surface, as clean as you possibly can, and allow a full day of drying time.

add a final finish

- **Apply two coats** of latex polyurethane—the type that is formulated specifically for floors. The polyurethane will be slippery for a time; choose a satin finish, and do not sand it. This should not be a problem if you are installing carpeting—or if your project isn't stairs or a floor. After two weeks, you can quickly wash the floor with dish detergent and water to reduce slipperiness.

WHEN YOU USE THE RUSTIC GRAINING FORMULA over a red base coat and high-light and age it further in the corners, you can render a believable interpretation of old American chestnut, as shown by this simple Colonial-style mantle.

Clair Bois for a Damaged Floor

paint saves the day

Replacing a wood floor can be costly. But this clair-bois treatment is both inexpensive and easy to do yourself.

If you're worried about ripping up old glued-down carpeting because the wood floor underneath it may be damaged, check out this fresh interpretation of a rustic wood technique. It's a great idea, especially if the floor is not worthy of refinishing in a traditional manner.

apply paint to the clean floor

1 **After removing** the carpeting and padding, sand the floor boards using 80-grit sandpaper. Then wash the floor; let it dry; and go over it again to clean up any dust or sanding residue. Take a clean, dry brush, and go over the entire floor, coating it with a flat latex paint in a medium-tone woodlike tan color. Apply the paint in a rather haphazard fashion so that you reveal some of the natural wood. This will add more interest to the final result of your project.

2 **Use water** to thin some flat off-white latex paint. Then brush the paint onto the floor in a random manner, but generally work in the direction of the wood's natural grain. This is another way to keep the final result interesting and fairly realistic.

create the "grain"

3 **Drag a wallpaper brush** back and forth through the wet paint. Paint brushes or steel wool would also do the trick, but the paint will dry quickly. That's why the large but easy-to-handle wallpaper brush is a good tool for the job.

Finish with three coats of polyurethane. For the first coat, tint the polyurethane with the burnt umber to straighten out any unevenness in the painting and to "weather" and mellow the look of the wood.

in the paint aisle

- 80-grit sandpaper
- Flat latex paint in off-white and medium tan
- Universal tint in burnt umber
- Polyurethane
- A brush
- A wallpaper brush

PLUS

- A floor vacuum
- Water
- Clean rags

CHAPTER 5

Shine, Shimmer,

all that glitters is not gold,

and *Glamour*

as you can see for yourself!

Manufacturers have perfected metallic paint to include user-friendly **premixed formulas** that are available in a **delicious and readymade** palette. How convenient! These paints and glazes **are effortless**, eliminating the need for tentatively mixing finely ground "mystery powders" into clear varnish. Now you can buy **metallic paints and glazes** in gallons, quarts, artist's acrylic, latex craft, and spray formulations at your local paint store. The **inherent shimmer** of metallic paint will lend **instant fabulosity to walls**, enhancing room proportions while quietly, or not so quietly, articulating the **luxuriousness of shine.**

WHAT A WAY TO GO! Applying metallic silver paint to the interior face of a pair of front doors adds instant glamour to this entry hall. The recessed spotlights enhance the sparkle by bouncing light off the surfaces.

the projects

Exactly two seconds after I dipped my paint stick into a rich bronze, I knew I was in love. If you try some of these projects, you'll know what I mean. When combined with unexpected undercoat colors, with relaxed over-glazing techniques, or in artful interpretations on their own, metallic paints allow the novice and the experienced decorator to render wall

bling underfoot

a spritz of glitz

metallic circles

and furniture treatments that deliver just enough of an extra touch to make them special while not over the top. For small pursuits, metallic craft paints and spray formulations are alternatives that can erase years of wear and lend sophisticated elegance to furniture, lamps, small art pieces, and accessories. So, are you ready? Then bring on the bling.

shimmery strié

Bling Underfoot

paint saves the day

A deep stain looks rich on a floor, but you can step it up with a glamorous, glittering accent.

I used a super-simple precut mylar stencil that I applied in a sophisticated metallic. (For information about ebony finishes, see Chapter 8, "Floors with Flourish," on page 148.)

in the paint aisle

- Measuring tape
- Acrylic metallic craft paint
- Blue painter's tape
- Precut mylar stencil
- Stencil brush
- Water-based polyurethane
- Clear shellac (optional)

PLUS

- Chalk
- Paper towels

plan your design

1 Measure the floor, and map out your design. Include the entire cut edge of the stencil in the math—not just the design itself. Use chalk to note every place where you will stencil the motif on the floor with an "X." This will serve as a registration mark that you can use to position the template repeatedly over the floor **(1a and 1b).**

apply the motif

2 Position the stencil over the registration mark, and secure it to the floor using blue painter's tape.

3 Pour a dollop or two of metallic paint onto a paper plate. Dip a stencil brush into the paint, and immediately offload a bit of it onto the clean side of the plate. You want to make sure to apply the paint evenly and not too heavily onto the floor surface. Too much paint will seep under the template.

4 Pounce the paint onto the template **(4a).** Use a paper towel to remove excess paint before lifting and repositioning the template **(4b).**

add a finish

5 Apply two coats of water-based polyurethane to the entire floor. If the design is elaborate and you want to be absolutely sure the polyurethane will not act as a solvent on the water-soluble acrylic paint, first brush a thinned coat of clear shellac over the design. Do not sand between coats.

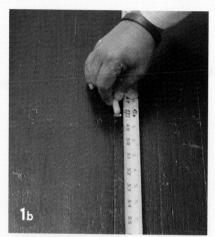

A Spritz of Glitz

paint saves the day

Tag-sale maple nightstands get a quick but glamorous lift from silver metallic spray paint.

Work outdoors or in a well-ventilated area. Use sheeting or plastic to make sure that you and the piece are protected from the wind and that any overspray will not drift onto nearby walls or other surfaces.

in the paint aisle

- Alcohol-based primer in white
- Universal tint in blue
- Metallic spray paint in silver
- 220-grit sandpaper
- Tack cloth
- Small utility brush
- Denatured alcohol
- Clear paste wax or clear latex polyurethane in a gloss finish

prepare the tables for paint

1 **Sand the pieces lightly** with a 220-grit sandpaper, and then dust them using a tack cloth. At this point, I also painted the tabletops white.

mask the tabletops, and apply a base coat

2 **If you have painted the tabletops** another color, protect them with plastic or newspaper; I used a plastic trash bag.

Use any shade of blue as a base coat for the "silver" finish. I tinted the primer with a drop of cobalt blue. That way it serves as both the primer and the base coat.

apply the metallic coat

3 **Shake the can** until the rattling stops. Then test your spray skills and the nozzle flow on a scrap of cardboard or newspaper.

4 **Beginning at the top,** depress the nozzle to begin to spray. Keep moving as you apply the paint to the piece. If the nozzle clogs or spits, turn the entire can upside down to clear it, and then continue.

If you miss a spot, allow the rest of the paint to dry. Then spray the missed area with a quick shot of paint.

5 **Apply clear paste wax** or clear latex polyurethane in a gloss finish. Each will alter the resulting shine somewhat and prevent you from touching up in the future. The metallic spray paint can wear well if it's left unfinished. But then you should never use ammonia- or citrus-based cleaning products on it.

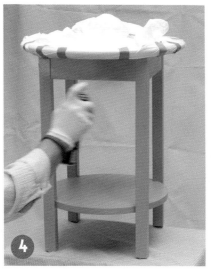

Shimmery Strié

paint saves the day

Plain white-painted paneling can look a little "been there done that." Adding cool blue-green color with a hint of shimmer can change it from beat to beautiful.

Because the existing paint was in good shape, I let it serve as the base coat. The paneling provided a logical place to start and stop, so the drag created by the flat-finish base paint could be worked into the strié. (If the wall needs a new base coat, apply a mid-sheen or eggshell finish in a color that is paler than that of the metallic paint.)

be a pro

BACK AND FORTH IS A NO-NO
Before you begin, practice moving up and down the surface in one continuous stroke with your brush. Familiarize yourself with your technique, making sure your hand and arm can comfortably move through the glaze mixture in a continuous stroke as you come down the ladder. Honestly, it is impossible to apply enough metallic paint to an 8-foot wall in one stroke and in one direction from the top to bottom. So, beginning below the ceiling, stopping short of the base, and finally blending it all together will keep the final results looking consistent. A second drag with a dry brush from top to bottom will even the finish.

in the paint aisle

- Ready-mixed latex metallic paint in silver
- Universal tints in Thalo Green and Prussian Blue
- Latex paint conditioner
- Painter's tape
- 4-inch natural-bristle brushes
- 220-grit aluminum oxide sandpaper

PLUS

- Dusting rags, dry rags
- Mixing buckets

design consult

HAUTE GLOSS WALLS

If you want a little luxury, you're going to need a little shine. The rewards of achieving a truly superior high-gloss finish with paint is diminished somewhat by the sheer drudgery of getting it done. The devil is in the preparation of the surface, which must be flawless, followed by the fiddling and fussing over the finish coats. For walls, buy the absolute best high-gloss 100-percent acrylic latex paint you can find in a color you love—with a capital L. After all that work, you will want to live with it for a long time.

sand; mix; and begin painting

1 After lightly sanding the walls, dust them, and then mask any molding and trim.

Stir the metallic paint well. Be sure to mix everything from the bottom of the can into the paint. I like to use two stir sticks or a big old spoon to mix metallics. These paints need good deal of stirring.

Pour off nearly enough for the project into a clean mixing bucket. Add a few drops of the Thalo Green and Cobalt Blue universal tints in equal proportions until you achieve the not-quite blue, not-quite green color. Add some of the silver reserve if the color is too intense. Then thin the mixture a little with latex paint conditioner (½ cup per gallon). Do not use water, which will dull the paint's sheen.

One-half gallon of tinted and thinned metallic mixture will cover about 400 square feet.

Beginning about a foot below the ceiling or crown molding, apply the metallic mixture to the wall surface in a series of long, continuous strokes; do not brush back and forth. Stop short—about 4 inches—of the base of the wall.

fill in unpainted areas, and finish

2 Reload the brush with a small amount of the metallic mixture, and fill in the untreated area at the top of the wall. Blend it into the already painted area in a continuous downward stroke.

3 Apply a small amount of paint to the uncovered 4 inches or so at the bottom of the wall. Again, blend this new paint into the already applied area, pulling up the brush in one straight motion.

With a dry rag, wipe any excess paint from the brush, and in one continuous stroke from top to bottom, lightly drag the brush through the paint from the ceiling or crown molding to the base trim. This final stroke, which is meant to organize and even up the mixture, will enhance the strié effect by revealing more of the base color. Be careful not to dillydally; metallic paint sets up fast.

Dampening the bristles in clean water will remove more of the applied metallic mixture and reveal more of the base color, making for a little more work and an equally remarkable result.

METALLIC WALL TILES are striking in this kitchen—but on a wall this size, you are looking at *mucho dinero*. Metallic paint would be just as dramatic and a lot more affordable. Use metallic paint on walls in a room where either natural or artificial ambient light will reflect on the surface.

be a pro

BRUSHES

I've read all the manufacturers' instruction booklets, researched all the information the online DIY tipsters offer, and listened intently to the wisdom other working pros have to offer on the subject of metallic paint. Nonetheless, you cannot apply metallic paint to a wall with a roller. Only one thing will do: one big, soft natural-bristle brush that is completely devoid of specks of dirt or debris. The ones pictured here are my favorites.

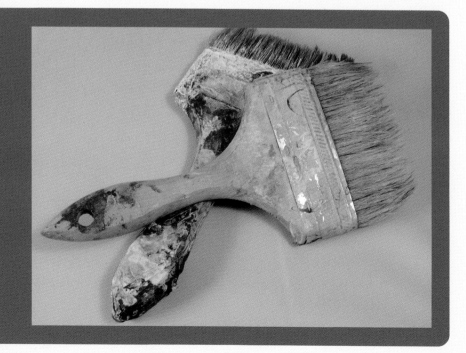

Just a Glimmer of Shimmer

in the paint aisle

- Assorted metallic pens
- A drill

PLUS

- A yardstick
- A pencil with an unused, clean eraser

paint saves the day

A large expanse of uneven walls can be a decorating nightmare. A simple graphic can camouflage the problem and add a mod metallic detail in a New York minute!

This project was made easier thanks to a super-friendly invention, the metallic paint pen. If you lack the skill to letter or line with a brush, these pens will do the trick. They make quick work of the circle motif here, which would have been tedious to stencil in such a random fashion. The pens are available in water and oil formulations, and drying times vary. While the pens themselves do not last very long, the work created with them will, particularly if you set it with a fixative. Crystal-clear spray fixatives will do, as will shellac or a clear glazing liquid. If you can find a solvent-based felt metallic pen, which is the type I used, it's a one-shot, washable, and durable deal.

draw the circles

1 **Drill holes all along a yardstick,** paint stick, or any other stick you happen to have around that suits your measure. Your circle will become twice the size of the space between whatever two holes you choose for the project. You can also make circles of different sizes this way.

2 **Note the center hole,** and secure it to the middle of the surface with a pencil eraser. Place your maker in the representative measurement hole, and make your circle.

3 **If you are right handed,** begin the circle with the marker under your left arm in the 6 o'clock position **(3a)** and work your way around in a circle, clockwise **(3b, 3c, 3d).**

be a pro

CIRCLE MAKING

You might have seen on YouTube some of those folks who can draw a perfect circle freehand every time, some with their eyes closed. It's a nice trick, but the rest of us will need our eyes and a jig of some sort. When a compass won't do, I like to use the stick method, demonstrated here. Using a string method is a little better for small areas near trim or for gigantic circles, especially ones applied on the ceiling. Tie a knot in a piece of twine. Secure the string to the surface using a pushpin, and attach the marker to the other end of the string—and around you'll go.

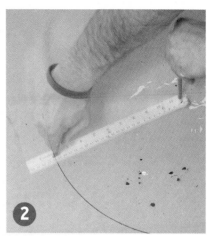

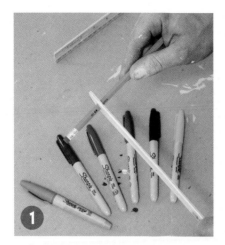

High-Gloss Walls, a Master Class

the preparation

Prepare the room for a big mess; make sure the room is very clean and well ventilated; and get prepping. Flawless preparation is an absolute must for high-gloss paint. Shine a bright light directly on the walls, and note all the imperfections with a sticky note or blue painter's tape. Fill the imperfections in the walls with drywall joint compound, or use wood filler on paneling. Once dry, sand the filler smooth using 220-grit sandpaper and recoat as needed. Caulk all the edges prior to priming. Tape and cover interferences, but do not tape the edges of ceilings, window trim, or base trim.

the primer

Sand previously painted walls and ceilings using 220-grit sandpaper on a pole sander. Spot-prime any incidental wall repairs with a quick-drying primer; dust the walls with a broom or a dust mop; and follow with a coat of full-bodied primer. This type of primer takes a long time to dry, has a lot of hide, and can conceal imperfections, such as brush strokes and track marks, in an existing poor paint job.

Full-bodied primers are formulated to be heavy, so don't thin them. Ask your paint dealer to shake the can. Then stir it until you can't believe you're still stirring it. In other words, stir it for a long time.

Start working at the top; cut in everything with a good brush; don't skip any areas; and allow for a good dry, which, according to my experience, is two hours longer than the label suggests.

Finally, sand the surface using 220-grit sandpaper, and then go over it thoroughly using a tack cloth. Be sure to clean the dust from the top of the base trim, the windows, and anywhere else it may settle.

the paint

High-gloss walls require first-class paint treatment, which means no tape, the best brushes, and the best rollers. Don't forget to work toward the light source. If you are rendering a high-contrast application, give the trim edges a quick scoring so the paint can float into the edge and will not need a lot of brushing. Cut in at least a foot beyond the trim and details with the brush, followed by a nice slow roll with a pink or

ASTUTE COLLECTORS of fine lacquer and japanned pieces (opposite top) may shudder at the naivety of this approach, but the critics would have a hard time demeaning a piece as lovely as the paisley beauty.

A MISHMASH OF FURNITURE (opposite bottom) is transformed into an important collection when you restyle it using high-gloss paint. Finish with multiple layers of glaze and a few coats of a high-quality paste wax rubbed down well, and oh my! How beautiful is that?

TRIM, DOORS, RAISED PANELS, and other architectural details (above) look as refined as a perfect Windsor knot when you render them in a gloss treatment. High-gloss proprietary colors appear just a bit more elegant than semigloss finishes. High-gloss paints are more durable and washable, too, making them a smart choice for busy areas around the house.

GLOSSY CEILINGS always add height and interest to a room (right). In this finished-attic space, the reflective quality of the paint enhances the natural light entering from small windows.

white short nap roller on a heavy cage. The trick to high quality is the pace, which is s-l-o-w—not too much paint on the roller, not too much paint on the wall, and a slow and steady application.

Once the paint is dry, only you can know whether you have reached the desired level of gloss, which will be a product of the paint quality, the application technique, and the color. Darker colors will have the least amount of shine. If you desire more, wet-sand the wall using 200-grit wet/dry sandpaper, then apply another coat of the high-gloss paint.

High-Gloss Floors

Building up a deep, high-gloss finish with polyurethanes or varnish is exacting work, and deciding what finish to use can be maddening. When you're narrowing down what product is right for the job, there are a few things to keep in mind.

Oil-based products dry slowly and tend to yellow or "amber" a little. The yellowing intensifies when the finish is covered and away from the light, such as under an area rug. But these finishes can be waxed, have the highest and most even sheen, feel good underfoot, and possess a nice "hand," which means they feel good to the touch.

Water-based, acrylic, and water-borne (another type that is distinct from water-based formulations) polyurethanes cast a little blue over dark surfaces. They dry quickly but do not level up (dry as evenly) as well as oil-based polyurethane. However, these finishes don't get yellow, either.

Water-based floor finishes may often be slippery, are not as nice to the touch as oil-based finishes, and cannot be sanded down as smoothly. But water-based products usually have the least-offensive odor, and some are highly durable.

Here are a few tips for selecting finishes:

- If the room is sunny and the painted work is dark, choose an oil-based polyurethane or varnish with a UV protector.
- If the floor is a vibrant color, use an oil-based polyurethane or varnish. Add a few drops of high-gloss oil-based paint that matches the paint color and a tiny drop of green universal tint to counteract yellowing. (Japan driers add a purple tone to varnish, which will be noticeable over paler colors.)
- If the room is sunny and the floor is pale or white, use a water-based, crystal-clear, high-gloss urethane. Follow the manufacturer's instructions carefully if you plan to use a water-based polyurethane over stained wood.
- Sand the polyurethane between coats, and wipe up with a clean tack cloth. How much of this you can bear is a highly personal decision, but somewhere between two and seven coats should do the trick. Do not sand the last coat.

These guidelines also apply to finishing wood cabinets and wood furniture pieces.

WHEN COMBINED WITH INTERESTING TECHNIQUES that enhance the contrast and soften the overall look, small spaces, such as this bathroom (left), will shimmer with style. The link to other shiny or metal surfaces in the room is another effective design device.

HIGH-GLOSS FLOORS look clean, clean, clean. A bold overall pattern, (opposite), is not always noticeable underfoot, but the shine adds to the play, catches the light, and is deceptively easy to dust.

TO TURN A GLASS-TOP TABLE into something extra special, use a little black and brown glass paint on the surface before you spray on "mirror" paint. The results will look exactly like a beautiful vintage piece (left).

YOU CAN HIT SOME LAVISHLY HIGH DESIGN NOTES in bronze, pewter, silver, gold, or platinum, but who could have guessed that today, even a "mirror" can come in a can (opposite)?

Metallic and High-Gloss Spray Paints

shake, rattle, and roll

Modern spray-paint formulas can deliver convincingly perfect representations of expertly plated metal finishes with which you can rescue door knobs, lighting fixtures, hinges, incidental hardware, or drapery rods. Or try them to render some fabulous art pieces out of wood cuts or cut foam core sprayed to look like chrome.

Find yourself an old violin, an odd chair, or some other sound piece of furniture, and give it the high-gloss spray paint treatment. Almost instantly, you will have a new, modern, fresh, and luxurious-looking something—provided you make the effort to achieve the flawless, near bone-hard surface preparation. Before you spray paint, remember: you must ready and prime any surfaces that are grainy, porous, chipping, peeling, or in any way uneven. Having made the effort and seen the results, however, you and other impulsive quick-change artists will love to reach for what the pros refer to as the "rattler can."

be a pro

A JIGGING BY ANY OTHER NAME

You can call it "jigging" or you can call it "rigging;" I call it "propping up." It makes no difference to me what you call it as long as you do it. Anything to be sprayed needs to be on a clean surface (newspaper is perfect). You also need ventilation, and the place should be warm—really warm. I do my spraying outside, in between the doors of my shed; the doors protect the piece from any wind, and I can move the piece off the propping and into the clean, newspaper-strewn shed to make room for the next. Before you have protected all the surfaces you do not wish to paint, prepare the back, underside, and leading edge of your piece, all of which you will spray first, propped up above the newspaper with wood, cardboard, or anything clean you don't mind getting overspray on. Do not put your piece on the lawn or on top of the trash can, and don't hold the thing in one hand and spray it with the other—and no—I do not care how they do it on TV. Dust is the enemy, drips are the enemy, and the unpainted underside of anything is wrong; take your time, and make it right.

getting it right

SPRAY PAINT HAS EXCELLENT ADHESION PROPERTIES. Some are lacquers, some are acrylic, and others have names I cannot spell. Accept that you are not going to get anywhere near the pigment-volume concentration in any other manufactured paint product available to the do-it-yourself market. You can use whatever happens to be on sale and is available in a color you like. But I warn you, do not spray different brands over one another without carefully reading the labels to be sure the solvent bases are compatible.

Because spray paint is somewhat expensive, consider the existing color of the piece and your intended result. If you have a long way to go (say, black to white), use a tinted primer—one that is as near to the finished color as possible. Alcohol-based primers are generally the most reliable under high-gloss spray paint. I would not recommend using spray paint over anything painted in oil-based enamel. If you are not sure, prime to be safe. There's nothing wrong with a quality spray primer for small projects, but they fly out of the can unbelievably fast. Try it out on something before you get started. Once the primer is dry, sand it thoughtfully. For the finest result, work up to a 200-grit wet/dry paper used wet; then dry-sand; and finally, clean the object or surface using a tack cloth.

Spray paints vary somewhat, and with a little experimenting you will find the brand that suits you best. Rattle the can with a good long shake and be sure the paint or whatever you are spraying is not cold. Dip the can into a bucket of warm water to ensure an even coat. Afterward, save the nozzles—they are often interchangeable, which can be a good thing when one clogs. It's probably worthwhile to test your performance on a piece of cardboard. Holding the can straight and at a 90-degree angle to what you will be spraying, keep the stream about a foot from the surface, and go. You will have an accurate impression of volume and an idea of how the paint lays onto a surface and whether it runs. Let's get glossy now!

CHAPTER 6

Pattern...

paintastic ideas for adding

Panache for Pennies

pizzazz using graphic patterns

Adding pattern can give a much-needed **visual boost** to a room. Extravagantly **taped** and executed, **boldly painted** pattern can also add **character and scale** to a space or distinction to a piece of furniture. Painted weaves that resemble **linen or grass cloth**, on the other hand, can make more **subtle statements.** (For more ideas along these lines, See Chapter 7, "Texture, A Nice Touch," page 132.) If you mix up the tools and allow the **color combinations** to **sing**, your patterns will defy examination and be **the talk of the town.**

UNEXPECTED WIDE HORIZONTAL STRIPES move the eye around this room. The subtle palette, however, prevents this bold graphic element from overpowering the space.

the projects

Few patterns can rival the classic, tailored appeal of a tone-on-tone stripe, and it's easy to do. I painted "Sophisticated Stripes" in a modern horizontal pattern to contrast with a dining room's antique furniture. Varying the mechanics of getting stripes on a wall will depend on the architecture of the room, the level of perfection you require, and the style

sophisticated stripes

be square

new room for old games

subtle and sublime
brushed blue weave

statement you wish to convey. Intermix some classic glazing techniques, vary the widths, and play with the palette; stripes can add a lot of style inexpensively, especially if you can apply them over existing paint that is in good condition.

Another way to add a wow factor to plain walls is with a big, bold grid, something you usually expect to see on a floor. Here, I rendered the look in warm green and white. But the stripes' impact is the result of their large size. This is not a look for the faint-hearted!

elegant ebony stripes

Taping is the key to creating stripes and grids, but I took it a step further in a whimsical game room where I painted backgammon and scrabble boards over a glazed and grained wall. The latter two techniques are applied to a pretty bedroom in this chapter. It features handsome trimwork and soft, grass-cloth inspired painted walls.

Finally, an ebony-striped chest of drawers is an easy project that takes just a day to accomplish.

Sophisticated Stripes

be a pro

EASY DOES IT
When you're masking the unglazed stripes, try using the tape as a plumb line, burnishing the top and allowing the roll to drop straight to the floor.

paint saves the day

Tone-on-tone glazed horizontal stripes offer an interesting counterpoint to vintage furnishings.

When you tackle this project, it's important to measure the entire room and spend a little time with the calculator to arrive at a stripe width that fits best. Perfection at the corners is a good thing; endeavor to end at each corner with a full stripe. Make small adjustments above windows to even things out if need be, or cheat by adjusting the width of the stripes at small intervals—they don't all have to be exactly the same, just perceptibly so. Plan a design in which the stripes vary drastically if the proportions of the room make it difficult to create a design.

measure
and make the stripes

- **Measure the height of the wall** to decide on the width and number of stripes you will paint. In this case, the stripes are 11 inches wide, more or less. Starting at the ceiling in one corner, move down the wall and make pencil marks at even intervals. Move to the next corner and do the same. Line up and connect the opposing marks using faint pencil dashes. Make sure your lines are even using a level. If you ahve help, a chalk line works, too.

- **Place a sticky note** on alternate stripes, which you will not glaze. Mask the inside edges of these stripes, from top to bottom, with tape. Check your measurements again, and then lightly burnish the tape with a rag.

apply the glaze

- **Mix a heavy latex glaze** consisting of 2 parts pink paint, 4 parts glaze, and 1 part water. Stir it well. Using a brush or foam roller, apply the glaze to the center of each stripe just short of the tape; then soften and "walk" it over the tape's edge using cheesecloth. Use a dry brush to lightly pounce the glaze neatly into the edge at the ceiling line and at the base trim.

- **Remove the tape,** pulling toward the wet glaze before it dries completely; then clean any bleeding with a dry rag. If there is a lot of bleeding, hold a painter's guide on the edge of the wet stripe, and whisk over the area with a dry brush.

in the paint aisle

- Measuring tools
- A level
- Brown paper tape or long blue masking tape
- Eggshell or matte finish latex paint in beige
- Latex paint in any color
- Glazing liquid
- Mineral spirits
- Assorted utility brushes
- Mixing containers and buckets

CAREFULLY WORK the paint into the corners and align the stripes perfectly for a professional result (above).

be a pro

FINESSE WITH STRIPES
It's hard to believe you can improve upon perfection, but for incontrovertibly expert results, apply a very thin, very matte, very pale scumble glaze over the entire striped wall surface. (For information about scumble glazes, see "The Classics," on page 12.) This will level out the sheen and add depth to the stripe while diffusing the edges ever so slightly. Walls finished in this manner feel and look exquisitely feminine, owing to the gauzy quality of the glaze—especially in a soft color.

be a pro

OIL-BASED GLAZES

You can use oil-based glazes for stripes, but the extra dry time slows down the project considerably. Oil glazes need to dry overnight before you can tape. A time-saving trick for horizontal stripes is to tape and glaze alternating stripes using latex glaze colors. Later, recoat the dry latex stripes with a simple, pale all-over oil glaze, working from the top to the bottom of the wall.

BE CREATIVE and turn an odd structural element into a design feature. A good example is this rhythmic pattern of aqua stenciled circles on the soffit, above. The hip three-color stripe is a visually powerful vertical element in this windowless room, as well, adding amusement and height without overpowering the space.

PRETTY IN PINK Glazed tone-on-tone stripes sidestep the often saccharine look of an all-pink room, right. It's a motif that has staying power because it's as suitable for a tot's room as it is for a teenager's hangout.

design consult

DESIGN-WISE, THERE IS SOMETHING DECIDEDLY MODERN ABOUT HORIZONTAL ELEMENTS, so if you're starting out in a big beige box of a room, stripes will enhance a contemporary look and add remarkable architectural interest. For height, graduate the size of the striped panels. Take the example of a wall with an 8-foot-high ceiling. Beginning at the bottom of the wall, make the first two stripes 14 inches high, followed by: one 13-, two 12-, one 11-, and finally, two 10-inch stripes. They'll look swell if you mix up the colors and have a little fun. Keep in mind that "builder's beige" flat latex paint is a suitable base for heavy latex glazes, saving time and money on the prep work.

A New Room for Old Games

paint saves the day

In a room that needs to look playful, a variety of techniques, including glazing and graining the walls and painting two whimsical gameboards, do the trick. Your turn!

As in strié, dragging a brush, steel wool, or more modest tools, such as notched plastic or cardboard, through a glaze will produce sophisticated linear effects. The magic really gets going when you render the manipulations in layers, in tooled combinations, or in a unique taped pattern as shown here in a super-big backgammon and scrabble-inspired painted wall.

in the paint aisle

- Measuring tools
- Latex paint in eggshell-finish cream and flat-finish golden brown
- Artist acrylic paint in black
- Latex glazing liquid
- Brown paper tape
- Rubber graining comb
- Permanent art marker
- Lettering stencils
- Stencil brush
- Brushes, buckets, rags

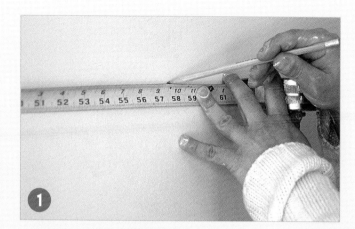

measure and mask the triangles

1 **Paint the entire room** in a cream-color eggshell latex paint.

Measure and, using the lightest pencil you can find, mark a horizontal line 12 inches below the ceiling and mask it off around the entire perimeter of the room. (Later, you can stencil or paint the scrabble-board letters to this area or band at the top of the wall.)

2 **To establish the elongated backgammon triangles,** measure each wall and divide it into equal segments. Make a light dot at the beginning and end of each segment just below the band. At the bottom of the wall, make a light dot at the halfway point of each segment. To mask the triangles, connect the dots; beginning at the left corner of the wall, run a line of brown paper tape, at an angle, down to the first pencil mark at the bottom of the wall. Then run a line of tape from the bottom point up to the second dot at the top. When you've masked each triangle, go over the tape and burnish it well.

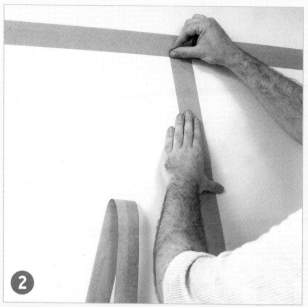

apply the glaze

3 **Apply a glaze** of 4 parts latex glazing liquid, 2 parts golden brown latex paint, and 1 part water to the wall with a brush. Work in an even, loose strié fashion. Take care at the corners and edges, and cover the wall surface evenly.

4 **Drag a rubber graining comb** through the wet glaze in a spirited, wobbly fashion to add a rhythmic wavy pattern to the triangle. Remove the tape immediately, pulling it toward the wet glaze, and then clean any bleeds with a dry rag.

(continued on page 122)

(continued from page 121)

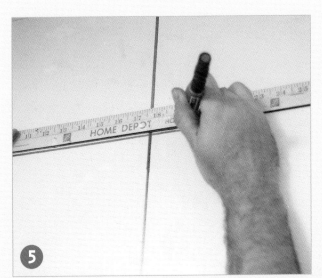

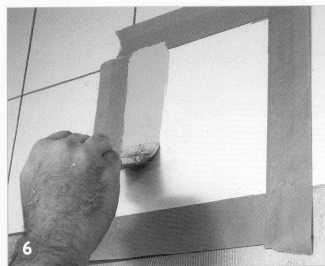

create the scrabble board

5 **Divide the 12-in.-deep ceiling band** in half horizontally. Using a square and a permanent art marker, draw 6 x 6-in. boxes on the wall inside this area.

6 **Mask the outside edges** of the boxes to which you plan to add color, and then paint them.

7 **After the paint dries,** use a stencil and artist's acrylic black paint to add the scrabble letters.

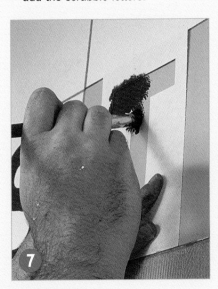

how to notch a squeegee

- To notch a squeegee expertly, remove the screws that hold the rubber part in place.
- Tape the long side of the rubber, leaving the length of the notches exposed. Using a ruler and pen, mark off the desired measurement for your notches, and note each alternating notch with an "x."
- Remove the notched-out areas. Reassemble the tool.

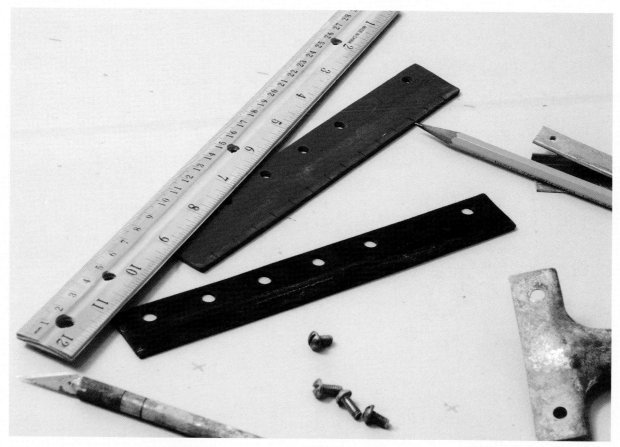

Be Square

paint saves the day

Big, bold painted squares provide the antidote to no trimwork, no art, no excitement, and no money!

If planning and taping skills come easy to you, have a go at big blocks, toned rectangles, or charming harlequins. As long as the surface is in good order, you can probably create a glazed geometric feature wall while the kids are in school. Follow the same tape and glaze methods described for "Sophisticated Stripes," on page 116, add a ragged or parchment glazing technique, and boldly flaunt your new skills. Before creating the grid for this project, I applied an eggshell-finish latex base coat in creamy white and let it dry overnight.

in the paint aisle

- Measuring tools
- Latex eggshell-finish paint in creamy white
- Brown paper tape or blue masking tape
- Universal tint in light green
- Chip brushes
- Cheesecloth
- Bucket

measure and mask the grid

1 Measure the wall to establish a suitable size for the grid. In this project, I divided the 8 x 12-foot wall into a 24 x 24-inch grid. Using a pencil, mark the wall lightly as a guide.

2 Apply brown paper tape to the entire length of the wall, cutting it back every 24 inches.

3 Reposition the tape (3a) to form the boxes of the grid **(3b)**. This is a time- and tape-saving trick that also keeps your layout neat.

apply the glaze

4 Mix a sharp latex glaze using 4 parts glaze, 2 parts water, and a green universal tint. Apply it to each alternating box with a brush, and then soften it with well-wrung wet cheesecloth before removing the tape. (Always pull tape toward the glaze, and clean bleeds with a dry cloth.) See how the contrast of paint and glaze lends a modern feeling to the finished look.

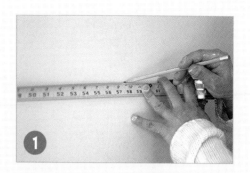

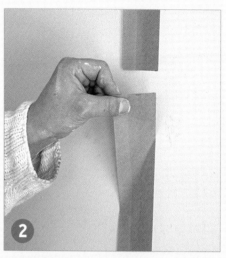

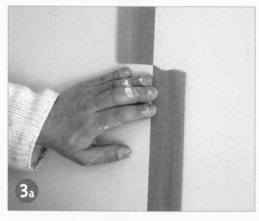

Subtle and Sublime
Brushed Blue Weave

in the paint aisle

- Latex paint in an eggshell or matte finish in blue (or alternative color)
- White latex paint
- Oil-based paint in white
- Latex glazing liquid
- Oil-based glazing liquid
- Two or more 4-inch China-bristle brushes
- Notched graining tool
- Synthetic brushes
- Mineral spirits
- Buckets

paint saves the day

People often complain that their rooms lack architectural details. But what if your problem is the opposite?

Handsome trim makes a big statement, so I used this subtle grass cloth-inspired technique to add color and pattern in a way that doesn't fight with the room's strong existing features.

create the vertical pattern

1 Apply two coats of latex paint in an eggshell finish. In this case, I chose a vibrant periwinkle blue. Let it dry, and then sand the walls well using 220-grit sandpaper.

Mix the glaze, which consists of 4 parts latex glaze, 2 parts cream-color latex paint, and 1 part water. Beginning at the top of the wall, and with the edges masked, brush on the glaze, and then drag a finely notched comb through it vertically. Wipe out the corners with a dry round art brush.

create the horizontal pattern

2 For the horizontal graining, combine 4 parts glaze, 2 parts white oil paint, and 2 parts paint thinner. Apply it as evenly as you can using a 4-inch China-bristle brush. Make sure to ready the brush with a good dunking and rubbing into and out of the mixed glaze before you begin.

While the heavy glaze is still wet, drag it horizontally end to end, using a dry 4-inch China-bristle brush **(2a and 2b).**

Note: If the surface seems too big for you to work through wet, tape a few breaks in any logical way. You can work the resulting line set up by the break.

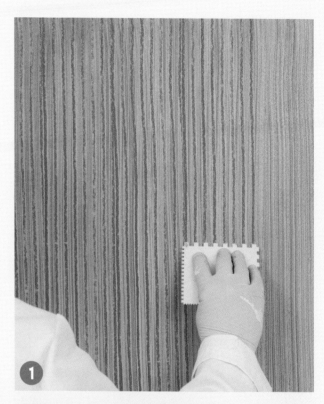

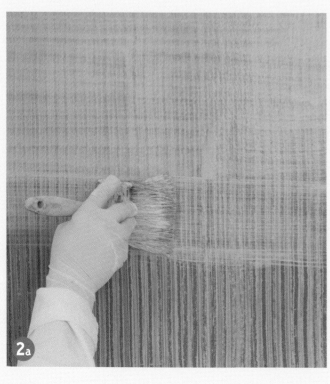

Elegant Ebony Stripes

paint saves the day

So, you have a plain chest that was something of a bargain, but it's nothing special.

Not to worry. You can turn it into a handsome accent piece by adding contrasting stripes to the wood finish. In this case, the rich ebony striping looks handsome next to the original pecan-color wood stain—and it was so easy to do. The trick is to make the stripes even using masking tape.

be a pro

CHANGING STRIPES

You can paint stripes on a piece of furniture in different hues, but if you do, let one color dry thoroughly before you mask the next stripe with tape.

Another snazzy idea is a metallic painted stripe. (For more information on applying metallic paint, see Chapter 5, "Shine, Shimmer, and Glamour," on page 92.) Or add a rich look with different color wood stains. Just remember that most wood furniture will require a protective finish.

prepare the surface

- **Once you have taped** your piece **(figure 1),** go over the exposed areas with 200-grit sandpaper; wipe them clean with a vinegar and water solution; and then go over them with a tack cloth. Then apply an alcohol-based primer followed by a wet sanding with 400-grit wet/dry sandpaper.

apply a base coat and glaze

- **Brush flat black latex paint** onto the exposed areas. (Japan paint is better suited to melamine and fiberboard pieces.) Add another coat if it's needed for coverage.

- **Mix a simple glaze** consisting of 4 parts oil-based glazing liquid and 1 part paint thinner. Make it a dark brown color using equal parts of raw umber, burnt umber, and burnt sienna universal tints. This heavy glaze runs, so keep watch for drips.

polish the finish

- **After the glaze dries completely,** rub the painted stripes with cordovan paste shoe polish. Add another coat. Then dunk a green kitchen scrubbing pad into soapy water; use it to polish the wax finish. Work in a circular motion; dry and buff the finish with a clean rag.

in the paint aisle

- Alcohol-based primer
- 200-grit sandpaper; 400-grit wet/dry sandpaper
- Flat latex paint in black
- Oil-based glazing liquid
- Universal tints in burnt sienna, burnt umber, and raw umber
- Cordovan paste shoe polish
- Mineral spirits or paint thinner
- Masking tape
- Brushes

PLUS

- Green kitchen scrubbing pad

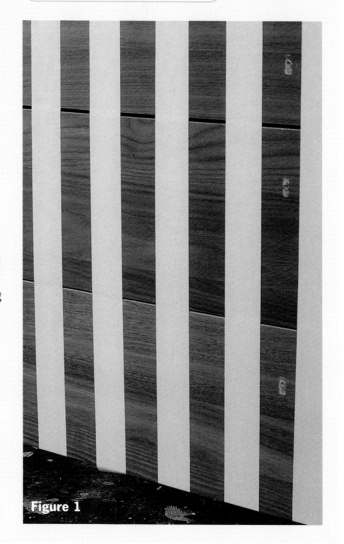

Figure 1

(continued on page 130)

(continued from page 129)

MAKE YOUR STRIPES NEAT with careful measuring. Also, don't forget to carefully burnish the edges of the tape to prevent seepage.

be a pro

HELPFUL TAPE TIPS

- To avoid bleeds and for sharp lines, rub down or burnish tape with a putty knife, or on delicate surfaces, a credit card.
- Avoid pulling the tape—it will stretch, twist, and get crooked.
- Always remove tape at a severe angle toward itself or in the direction of the freshly painted or glazed surface.
- Some tapes will bake onto a surface in a very sunny location, so keep a close watch.

And finally

- Try your best to tape in long runs, because having to remove a lot of little pieces of tape when you are waiting to see a final result makes some people grouchy. Take my word for it.

design consult

BASE THE NUMBER OF PAINTED STRIPES on the width of the piece and that of the tape. This chest here is about 36 inches wide, and I used 2-inch-wide masking tape. I used nine pieces of tape (18 inches), painted eight stripes (16 inches), and left the ends untouched (about 2 inches). To keep the the stripes as even as possible, I used long pieces of tape, running each from the back of the top of the chest onto and down the front. I taped the side panels separately.

tape, tape, and more tape

There are different types for different jobs. Here's my take on tape.

● PAINTER'S TAPE

This is the most reliable all-round tape for any job. There is both a blue and a green variety, and the manufacturers' recommended time for leaving it in place varies from either two days to two weeks. I have successfully pushed my luck for as much as a week or two with the blue. It comes in a few good sizes, won't tear the paint off the wall, and can be left on fully cured paint surfaces for as long as two weeks—a day or so on fresh paint. It bleeds more than the brown tape, twists when it runs free (as in stripes), and will take the finish off a polyurethane floor if it is left on longer than a couple of weeks. If you have taped and protected a freshly finished floor with this tape, note the date you will have to remove it.

● LOW-TACK TAPE

This is also called "safe release" or "artist's tape." It is of little use because it really doesn't stick to anything all that well. I find it helpful for a quick mask on a tacky painted surface, so I keep a roll handy.

● MASKING TAPE

Once upon a not-so-long-ago time, this was the only tape to buy. Often called "painter's tape" and recognizable by its beige color, it will stubbornly stick to glass, pull off the paint on walls, and dig into polyurethane finishes. But it is useful on cured trim paints, although the glue will sometimes dig into it. This makes for a nasty little lighter fluid scrub down to remove the glue. Yes, it is less expensive, and it is the only tape to use on brick, stone, and carpeting. I use it to label paint cans or tape down the lids. I really like it on fabrics and lampshades. Other than that, masking tape is an outdoors thing; keep it away from interior walls.

● BROWN PAPER TAPE

As pictured in many projects, this tape is the go-to product for most decorative artists. It burnishes well and renders the sharpest line. It can be a little temperamental on fresh paint; its 2-inch width can be a help or a hindrance. But I have left it on a painted floor for as long as a week. This is the easiest tape to cut, and finally, it doesn't stretch when you apply it in long, vertical loose runs. Brown paper tape can be a little difficult to find at your local paint dealer, but it is available from finishing suppliers.

● SPECIALTY TAPES

Striping tape is handy for grout and tiny pattern details. It is only available in a masking tape, so it will sometimes pull the paint from the wall, especially if the job is fresh and the primer is latex. However, striping tape is the only option for masking very narrow areas. Plan to do some fiddling with a brush on faux-stone grout lines after you pull off the tape. Buy a few different sizes to add tidy lines to a vinyl floor cloth or to stripe your furniture projects.

be a pro

LET'S GET THINGS STRAIGHT

You can hang a plumb line (or something heavy tied to the bottom of a string) from the ceiling near each corner of the room. Run a piece of blue tape up the wall, mimicking the plumb line. This will give you a dead-level vertical line from which to measure. A story pole is a handy thing when you're working alone (as I often am), and a laser level will do all of this figuring for you—if you know how to use one. (I do not.) For stripes, measure each wall; establish a logical width; and mark the measurements onto the wall along the top and bottom of the wall. Connect the dots with a plumb line, pole, long level, or chalk line. If you snap chalk lines, use either blue or white chalk; every other chalk color is too permanent and winds up in every inch of the work.

CHAPTER 7

Texture...

two deceptively easy techniques

a Nice Touch

can render great changes

If you want to make a room interesting, include **texture** in your mix of furnishings and finishes. Use it to add **interest and artistry.** Create a **vintage look** on walls or furniture. And on the practical side, texture **comes to the rescue** after a parade of quick fixes have subjected **your walls** to careless changes. After you spend a little extra time in this chapter, you'll realize that **joint compound** is a **beautiful thing**—especially when you apply a glaze or a color wash over it. It's **easier** than applying Venetian plaster. Then try a crackle finish, a **fascinating** technique that involves layering on and then peeling back color. Talk about **aging gracefully!**

RECALLING ANCIENT EVENINGS this rendering of age to the walls of a cozy niche enhances the mood of a far-off time and place.

the projects

Peels and crackles are the go-to techniques to create age and texture on furniture. You can find crackle medium in any craft store today, but what sets some of these finishes above others is good timing, patience, and a willingness to read and follow the manufacturer's instructions. Because I possess none of these attributes, I asked another artist,

textured joint compound

tooled texture

crackle finish

my friend Deidre, to prepare the extraordinary example of a crackle finish, which appears on pages 144–145. But before you get to that, I'd like to show you how to add texture to a wall using drywall joint compound. This is a relatively easy project that offers a creative way to camouflage damage on old walls or add the illusion of age to new ones.

TO CREATE THE ILLUSION OF AGE, you have to reproduce both the "feel" of an old surface and the way color fades unevenly over time.

Texturing with Joint Compound

paint saves the day

Damaged walls got you down?

Camouflage the offending surfaces with texture that you can add using joint compound. Your ability to exploit the forgiving nature of this technique will grow exponentially if you incorporate the textures into painted patterns, stenciled designs, or more elaborate inventions in delicious colors.

in the paint aisle

- Lightweight drywall joint compound
- A 6-inch taping knife
- A mud pan
- Clean bucket
- 220-grit sandpaper along
- Gloves and dust mask
- Cellulose sponge
- Universal tints or latex paints (optional)

apply joint compound

1 With the ceiling and trim taped and masked, load a fair amount of the compound onto the taping knife. Keep the big bucket covered to prevent drying. Holding the loaded tool at an angle that is comfortable, apply a thin layer of the compound to the wall in a counterclockwise direction and in one continuous pass to form a half circle.

2 Working clockwise this time, make another pass with the still-loaded taping knife to complete the circle. Continue covering the entire wall this way, alternating counterclockwise with clockwise motions to create indiscernible shapes and patterns with the joint compound.

If your base coat is meant to enhance your finished result, be sure it peeks out in a pleasing mélange of color and goop. Modify shapes or soften heavy areas using a well-wrung cellulose sponge dabbed this way and that on the wet compound.

At the ceiling and any edges where the compound and tape meet, apply a slightly thinner layer. Let everything dry. Before removing the tape, carefully score it where it meets the dry compound using an easy-to-hold, not-too-sharp tool. (A screwdriver is too long, while a cheese server, a dull paring knife, or one of those cute little jam knives works perfectly. I use a clam shucker.)

add color to the textured wall

3 Apply paint, a glazing technique, or a wash. I used three colors here: gray (60 percent), beige (30 percent), and off-white (10 percent).

Using a wet sea sponge, apply the first color to a portion of the wall surface in an entirely random fashion. Allow the wash (or paint or glaze) to drip and run.

4 With the largest brush you can manage, soften the media, "scrubbing" and pouncing it into the compound.

5 Apply the next color using the sponge, and then soften it with a brush.

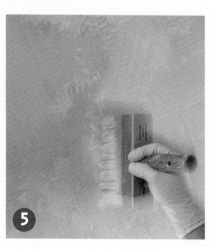

(continued on page 138)

(continued from page 137)

before you slap it on the wall

- Prepare the room for a big mess and test the surfaces to be taped. You won't have to burnish the tape, but you should score the edges after the compound dries. Decide where you'll begin and tape your way in and out of the corners. It's a big help to have a ladder that's tall enough to keep the mud pan within easy reach.

- Check the existing paint for tooth, or adhesion; rub your hand over the surface to see whether or not you can push it. If so, you can apply the compound directly to this surface. If your hand goes flying across the wall, the existing paint is too shiny and slippery to hold the compound unless you first apply a latex primer. Don't cheat—joint compound over a slippery base will crack. Adding a little white glue to the compound will help the problem, but only in a pinch. It's a great trick for outside corners, but adding white glue is not a good adhesion solution for an entire room.

- If you've never done this sort of work before, start in the middle of the wall and move around working from left to right and up and down. That way, your gradually improving technique will not be noticeable without careful scrutiny.

design consult

THE WORK GOES SURPRISINGLY FAST, particularly if the kids, a weekend guest, or anyone with arms can be cajoled to help. The training session can be brief—get the goop on the walls. Have some fun with your color choices, and if you need ideas, maintain a reference to natural materials, in this case, stone. Whenever you are feeling a little fearful about color, let Mother Nature inspire you.

Figure 1

Figure 3

Figure 2

A THREE-COLOR WASH
Applying it over unprimed compound belies the economy of time and effort **(figure 1)**. Left porous and completely unsealed, the compound will absorb each of the tinted wash colors unevenly and dry very quickly. It is an exhilarating technique that requires speed and confidence and beautifully replicates a dry, aged effect.

A WASHABLE COLOR WASH
Use a latex primer **(figure 2)** and then go over the compound with a color wash. The formula is made of thinned latex paint. To offset the lack of porosity in the compound, use a soft dry rag to chase drips and rub back the glaze here and there.

GLAZING AND TEXTURE
You can tint the glaze with paint or universal tints, **(figure 3)** and you can apply a single color or several. This is the best approach if your walls are high and you'll need time to get up and down a ladder. This glaze is the most washable.

be a pro

JOINT COMPOUND
All-purpose joint compound, which is sold in 2- or 5-gallon premixed quantities, and its lightweight alternative, are the best for the job. Avoid the quick-drying products, which are not necessarily a plus if this is your first try. Removing the top from a 5-gallon bucket is nearly a rite of passage. If you're strong enough to get it home, you're strong enough to get it open. Whacking a slotted screwdriver through the plastic holes with a hammer using every ounce of strength you've got will work, but there is a tool made specifically for the job. Buy it.

Tooled Texture

paint saves the day

When old wallpaper is too hard to remove or you just don't have the time, applying a tooled strié technique can come to your rescue.

This is also a handsome look for rooms with chair rails, as well as small halls and areas without too many little nooks and crannies. Tooled texture is a finish that has come into its own. Monochromatic modern spaces benefit the most from the addition of texture, as may new additions to older homes where you want to play down a little of the newness in order to blend it with the original house. You can tint the compound before it is applied, and then after it dries, prime and paint the wall or treat it to the same glaze or color-wash technique as a bladed joint-compound texture.

in the paint aisle

- Lightweight joint compound
- Large 12-inch taping knife
- Wallpaper brush
- Small brush with cut bristles

coat the wall with the compond

1 Apply the joint compound to the wall surface in a fairly even, near skim-coat fashion.

2 Beginning at the top, drag a wet wallpaper brush down through the wet compound to create the raised strié. If the wall is too long for one straight pass with the brush, work from the top down a little more than halfway; remove the brush and clean it. Begin again from the bottom, work up toward where you left off, and blend the two applications.

finesse tight spots

3 You can pull out corners, tight edges, and globs along the base or the ceiling using a small brush with bristles that you have cut short.

(continued on page 142)

(continued from page 141)

be a pro

USE THE BRUSH EFFECTIVELY

Use the entire bristle of the brush to create the strié. Get rid of any excess compound by dipping the bush into a bucket of clean water whenever necessary. For added dimension, you can place your hand flat over the bristles of the brush to push out more of the compound. Make an effort to find a comfortable level of drag to use on the brush, keeping in mind your hand will tire as the work progresses and the technique will appear different if you vary the pressure on the brush.

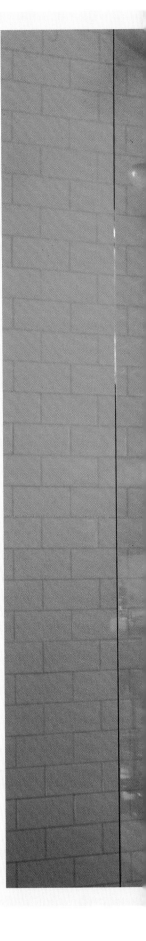

A VERTICAL COMPOUND-TEXTURE TECHNIQUE that was covered in (left) was the solution to restoring a hallway with old wallpaper.

THIS HORIZONTAL COMPOUND-TEXTURE TECHNIQUE (right) covers the wall surface in a bathroom. The background color is a dark brown. I tinted the compound with white paint. The strié reveals the brown base coat and gives the look of bark or grass cloth. A coat of clear glaze ensures that the finish will remain serviceable in a busy family bathroom.

Textured "Age"

paint saves the day

A crackle finish was perfect for this table made of richly toned wood, which was in perfect condition except for a battered top.

Instead of painting over the wood, a crackle is rendered directly on the wood surface. This is an unusual approach that adds an appealing dimension to this fascinating technique.

in the paint aisle
- Crackle medium formulated for furniture and walls
- Latex eggshell paint in vivid red
- 220-grit sandpaper
- A tack cloth
- Brushes
- Polyurethane
- Varnish or furniture wax

apply the crackle medium and paint

1 Remove hardware; then prepare the work area and piece for painting. Sand it lightly with 220-grit sandpaper, and go over it thoroughly with a tack cloth.

2 Apply a heavy layer of the crackle medium in one stroke and in one direction. Do not brush back and forth.

Following the manufacturer's instructions, leave the medium to set for the required length of time. Plan your timing strategy if the piece is large. It may be necessary to stagger the application of the medium to allow you the time to finish the areas that are ready for paint.

Apply the paint over the dry crackle medium, again working in one direction, no going back and forth. The paint should be applied heavily, but not so much as to cause peeling. In this case, "heavily" is the equivalent of a fully loaded brush dragged lightly over the surface until it no longer leaves any paint **(2a).**

Reload the brush, and working from where you left off, continue over the dry medium **(2b).**

add a top coat

3 The paint will begin to crack and craze in about five long minutes. Once the paint is completely dry, you can finish the piece with polyurethane, and then varnish or wax it for added protection.

(continued on page 146)

(continued from page 145)

design consult

GLAZING AND STAINING OVER A CRACKLE FINISH will add age to a surface or an object. The base coat is always evident in the result and should be selected to add dimension to the final look. The color choice is of particular importance when you will be applying a crackle or aging technique to small areas of a wall.

ANTIQUE OR NEW? It's hard to tell, judging by the "age" on this piece (above). Actually, the hutch is new, but you didn't hear it from me. Okay?

AN AGED TEXTURE (left), the result of spot crackling and an overall glaze, resembles an old peeling, painted stone wall.

VINTAGE CHARM, courtesy of a crackle finish applied over bead-board paneling (opposite), enhances a new bathroom's Victorian styling.

CHAPTER 8

Flooring
banish a damaged or boring floor

with Flourish
using paint and a dab or two of flair

Because hardwood floors are so desirable, the idea of covering them with paint **may seem crazy.** Forget that notion. If you have an old floor with boards that are worn too thin to sand and restain, you can **save them** with **paint.** Have you ever ripped up wall-to-wall carpeting only to **discover** a water- or pet-stained floor? That's another case for paint **to the rescue.** In this chapter, you'll find ideas and instructions for saving a wood floor—or wallet—from the brink of disaster with affordable paint and **priceless ingenuity.** The why of it all is as diverse as the how, but make no mistake, when properly done, a painted wood floor is **extraordinary.**

A CAPTIVATING PAINTED BORDER—applied freehand, but you can use a stencil—can be a decorative way to delineate space in an open-plan layout. It's also a charming device to perk up a tired hardwood floor.

the projects

Use the following projects as a guide with which to plan your own low-cost floor rejuvenations. All are painted with either a flat latex paint, artist's acrylic paint, acrylic craft paint, or Japan paint. Floor surfaces can be bold in style and color, so let your imagination run wild. Mix and match your painting, taping, stenciling, and fine-art skills; in the end, you will

paintastic in brown & tan

chic in black, white & gray

faux bois the bois

a modern grid

have a look no rug could ever rival. Lay out your inspirations on graph paper or make a sample if you're feeling unsure. Got any leftover latex paint in the garage? Use the palest color for the base coat, which you will apply over a primer as needed. The sheen will be determined by the final coats of the polyurethane finish you select.

ALLOWING THE EXISTING WOOD FINISH to become a part of the design creates an interesting pattern as the intricate grid magically appears in this big brushed plaid rendered on the bias. The semitransparent, thinned-down latex paints create interesting tones as they pass over each other to form yet another box.

Paintastic in Brown and Tan

paint *saves the day*

Badly water- and pet-stained floors are usually beyond repair—no matter how much sanding and bleaching you do.

If that's the case, and you don't want to cover or can't afford to replace a wood floor, an overall painted design is a creative solution. All it costs is the price of paint and a few days of your time.

in the paint aisle

- Mesh sanding screen
- Sanding sealer
- Flat latex paint in off-white and brown
- Universal tint in burnt umber
- Brown paper tape
- Blue masking tape
- Measuring tape, chalk-line box, and a square
- Satin oil-based polyurethane
- Paint thinner
- Brushes
- Tack rags/sandpaper/dusting brush

PLUS

- Professional sanding machine
- Broom or fiber-covered sweeper
- Buckets
- Pencils

sand the floor

1 Go over the entire floor, including the water-damaged area, using a professional sanding machine and a mesh sanding screen. Seal the raw, sanded wood with two coats of sanding sealer to isolate the stains.

Using a 4-inch brush, apply two coats of the off-white paint. Work in the direction of the floorboards and the wood grain. If you prefer to use a roller, cut in at the edges with a brush. Allow the paint to dry well (overnight) in order to receive the tape.

make the grid

2 Lay out a diagonal grid using a blue or white chalk line. You can expect some of the chalk from the grid to wind up in the work, but the blue will nearly disappear into the polyurethane finish.

Next, measure and mark up the pattern—in this case, 8 x 8-inch boxes—using tiny pencil lines that can be erased in case of a mistake. Do not lay out the pattern in chalk. Keep the floor as dust free as possible while you are working.

(continued on page 155)

BLUE AND WHITE is another classic color combination. For a high-contrast pattern, use the light color as the base coat and burnish the tape to avoid bleeding.

(continued from page 152)

3 **Tape the marked-up pattern** to protect or conceal the alternating off-white base coat. Notice that I cut the pointed edge of the tape neatly with a blade, and then burnished the tape to avoid excessive bleeding. Also, the overlapping edges form a square over one another when the pattern is precise—a nice check if the pattern starts to fall off as you work across the floor.

apply the paint

4 **Check that your layout appears straight.** Consider where to start painting, and how to move around while you're applying the alternating color—in this case, brown.

5 **Wait until everything is dry** before pulling up the tape, but do not leave it down longer than necessary. Pull it toward the fresh paint to avoid peeling. Pick off stuck pieces using tweezers or a straight razor. Then sweep the floor.

Apply three coats of oil-based polyurethane in a satin finish to the entire floor using a hog-hair natural-bristle varnish brush. (A lamb's wool applicator is handy for large floors.)

For the last layer, you can tint the polyurethane with burnt umber to add overall warmth to the floor.

design consult

A LARGE KITCHEN RENOVATION left large areas of flooring missing, and most of the floor that did exist was badly stained from a leaky old radiator. Pets, overflowing dishwashers, and holes from relocated plumbing all conspired to ruin the once solid and proud white oak floorboards. Because it was too costly to install an all-new floor, I replaced only the missing and damaged areas and finished all 400 square feet with a handsome technique.

More Chic Squares

paint saves the day

There is a limit to how many sandings a ¾-inch-thick floor can bear.

Too many owners, too many dogs, and too many overly zealous flooring contractors have decimated these once-lovely 100-plus-year-old wide-plank pine floors. Paint will protect what little is left of them while lending some shabby-chic charm to the room. The floor can always be painted over again if you want to make a color change or refresh the floor with a different design.

in the paint aisle

- Latex paint in black, white, and gray
- Latex satin-finish polyurethane
- 220-grit sandpaper
- Blue masking tape
- Tack cloths
- Large paint brushes

PLUS

- A dusting brush
- Measuring tape, chalk-line box, and a square
- Buckets
- Pencils

Before

Figure 1

Figure 2

mask and paint

- **Thin the white latex paint** by about 25 percent with water. Apply it as a base coat using a large brush and working in the direction of the floorboards. This layer should appear unfinished and nearly messy, revealing some of the old wood. Then mask the floor using blue tape if the flooring is uneven. **(figure 1)**

- **Thin the black and gray paints** by about 10 percent with water. Apply these colors side by side or randomly as shown in the photograph. Render them to look a bit worn like the base coat by coating the boxes with an uneven amount of paint.

lightly sand and finish

- **After the work dries overnight**, remove the tape. Fuss around a bit, sanding any heavy spots and adding more paint to areas that are too transparent. All of this work can be sanded hard—in the direction of the grain—if you want the floor to have a more-distressed look.

- **Vacuum, dust, and finish the floor.** Apply a coat of water-based, nonyellowing polyurethane, or use a mellower oil-based polyurethane, which you can tint and "dirty" by adding a little raw umber to it. **(figure 2)**

design consult

IS A HARDWOOD FLOOR only something on your wish list for the time being? Painted plywood subflooring is a temporary transitional fix that you may come to love too much to ever replace. And it's doable in just a weekend. Install standard ¾-inch 4x8-foot plywood panels. Cut them into a 4 x 4-foot grid, and glue them down using a liquid adhesive product to prevent squeaks. Then screw them in place using stainless-steel screws that you can remove later if you will use the plywood as a structural underlayment for another flooring material in the future.

Use a damp rag to wet the plywood and raise the grain; sand it using 220-grit sandpaper; and then apply one coat of sanding sealer.

Finally, paint your design. You can even render the look of a fine wood grain that will be hard to distinguish from the real thing! But be sure the nails are set, and fill any holes with wood filler.

CLASSIC STYLING AND UNDERSTATED COLOR join together outdoors to add a smashing look to a porch (top).

INTRICATE PATTERNS, INLAYS, AND PARQUET DESIGNS are easier to achieve rendered in paint (left). The paint has less of a tendency to bleed than stain, dries quicker, and is almost indistinguishable from stain.

A DIAMOND PATTERN (opposite) looks more formal and refined than a checkerboard, which is better suited to a country decor.

be a pro

PRISTINE JOB

Always wash and vacuum a floor thoroughly before applying paint or stain to it. This may mean cleaning it repeatedly if the floor is large and your work will extend over several days. Otherwise, any "schmutz" left on the surface will look like an imperfection in your finish.

Faux Bois the Bois

paint saves the day

We needed to replace some old wide-plank pine floorboards. This type of wood has a grain pattern that is hard to find and harder to pay for once you've found it.

I turned to a more practical solution—new ¾-inch-thick pine boards, planed to sit unobtrusively next to the original wide planks. A faux bois (fake wood) technique added 150 years of age to them in one afternoon.

in the paint aisle

- 3-pound cut orange shellac
- Denatured alcohol
- Universal tints in burnt sienna, raw umber, burnt umber, and Van Dyke brown
- Brown and black tube artist acrylic paint
- Fine art brushes
- Assorted chip brushes
- Oil-based satin-finish polyurethane

prepare to paint

1 Install the new boards, and then sand and vacuum them. Thin the denatured alcohol by 50 percent, and apply three coats.

create the "grain"

2 Squeeze some of burnt sienna, raw umber, burnt umber, and Van Dyke brown onto individual paper plates. Add a spoonful each of medium-brown and black acrylic paint to the plates.

Using a small fine-art brush, mix a small amount of burnt sienna with the brown acrylic and paint it onto the new pine to simulate the old wood's growth-grain pattern. Then whisk and blur it with a wet China-bristle brush, working in the direction of the grain.

Continue to re-create the old grain. This time use raw umber with the brown; then apply the next pattern using Van Dyke brown with the brown acrylic. Keep alternating the tints this way and always whisk and blur the pattern with a wet China-bristle.

3 Thin a small amount of shellac by 50 percent, and then tint it with a tiny amount of Van Dyke brown. Apply it over the newly "grained" boards. Follow with another shellac layer, thinned and tinted this time with a tiny amount of burnt sienna. Keep applying tinted shellac this way until the new wood begins to look close to the original.

Cut a potato or a piece of sponge and load it with the brown paint tinted with burnt umber. Use it to make random impressions that will resemble knots.

Soften the look with a gloved index finger, a paint stir stick, and the end of fine-art brush. This will "break the color" and "push" interest into the wood.

Apply up to two additional coats of tinted shellac as needed. Then finish the floor with three coats of oil-based polyurethane. Sand lightly between the first and second coats.

A Modern Grid

paint saves the day

Don't despair if you hate to measure, are bored by grids, or prefer to take a more colorful approach to a painted floor project.

If you choose colors that complement the room and keep the lines straight and the edges sharp, the design can be as stylishly random as you like with immeasurably smashing results.

in the paint aisle

- Flat latex paint
- Assorted artists acrylic colors
- Painter's tape in assorted widths
- 220-grit sandpaper, tack cloths
- Latex semigloss polyurethane

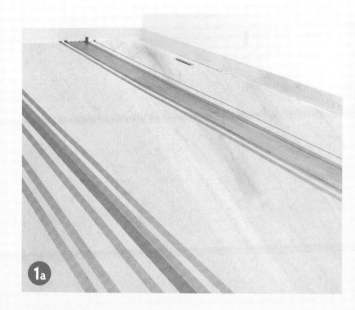

paint the floor

1 Sand and wipe the floor. This floor was newly installed unfinished maple and prepared for paint with a quick sanding and a coat of sanding sealer. (Maple is an inherently slippery hardwood, so a meticulous sanding would exacerbate this issue and remove the tooth needed for the paint layers.)

Paint the entire floor with two coats of latex paint using a brush. (I used neutral beige, but the choice is yours.)

Once the paint dries, tape your design in a straight, random pattern **(1a)**. Paint each taped area separately **(1b)**. Each color is painted individually; pull the tape immediately toward the wet paint.

finish the floor

2 Apply three coats of a semigloss latex polyurethane. Sand after applying the first and second coats for a flawless sheen.

design consult

IF AN AREA RUG REMAINS IN YOUR FUTURE, why not treat the floor to a unique and awe-inspiring border for now? You may cross the rug off your wish list altogether, or choose a size that lets you keep the border on display. Isolating the area to be painted in the border design eliminates the need to prep or polyurethane the entire floor surface, making ongoing or over-the-top design ideas easier to accomplish. Many borders are easy to render using stencils and tape. (See the photo that opens this chapter.)

CHAPTER 9

Solve it

is it magic?

with Color

no, it's pure and simple color

Adventurous color enthusiasts may be blessed with a curious nature or just good instincts. They can plan a perfectly balanced, **complex palette** without blinking while everyone else can only be **awestruck.** So many other times, however, people **struggle** with color. They test one after the other, invite opinion, and in the end, still go with the safety of beige walls with white trim. Because even a little dose of a **well-chosen color** can solve more decorating problems than a team of able carpenters—at a **fraction of the price**— why not go for it? Treat yourself to a quart of an **extravagant orange** or a **surprising purple** and see what happens.

A TANGERINE-COLOR partition helps to define space in this open-plan loft. It's a good choice for a dining area, as well, because it stimulates conversation and appetite.

What About It?

Most books published on the subject of paint and color begin with the ubiquitous color wheel and color models that explain that red, blue, and yellow are **primaries** and orange, violet, turquoise, and lime green are **secondaries.** But there's a more basic, visceral way for you to begin your adventure with color and that is to ask yourself, "What colors do I love?"

Do you remember the first time you were dazzled by color? It was probably while staring at the 48 delicious and perfectly arranged colors in your first box of crayons. If you had the big box of 64, you didn't have to settle for magenta; there was Tickle Me Pink and Cotton Candy, two among many scrumptious "new" offerings. Did you leave violet in the box because it was a favorite you wanted to save or did you simply prefer Mulberry?

This may seem a naive approach to introducing color theory, but it's worthwhile to reminisce about the cherished blue-purple you hid beneath the coloring book. And was it the Olive or the Pine Green you wore down to the nub?

For the professional and the novice, the **color wheel** is a tool for organizing, planning complex palettes, and perhaps most importantly, mixing colors. But you'll still need to choose your favorites. Done that? Then let's get started.

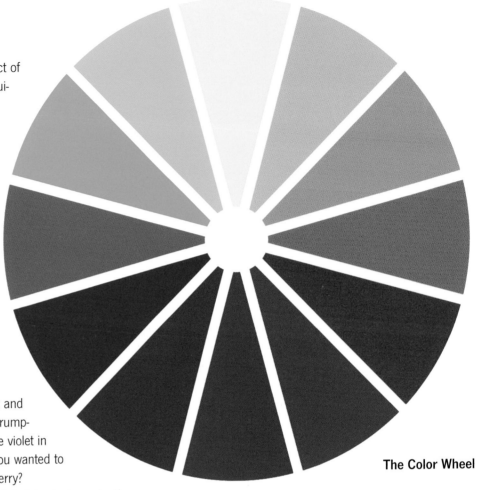

The Color Wheel

planning a palette

The position of the colors on the wheel will help you to choose fundamental combinations for a room. **Analogous** colors reside next to one another. Color schemes defined as analogous—green and yellow, for example—are generally considered calming and balanced. **Complementary** colors are opposite one another on the color wheel, in which case the same yellow would be paired with violet, but probably not as equals. These schemes are often the easiest to plan and pleasing in a home.

Monochromes are made up of varying shades of any one color. Again using yellow as an example, varying amounts of white can be added to the yellow. Tinted, or shaded, each version of the color would be discernible, while the overall scheme remains yellow. While a monochromatic palette is beautiful, life's little essentials—which could be anything from a new appliance to a coffee mug—can wreak havoc on it, as it falls flat when any other color is added.

To these three fundamental approaches, you can add more complex schemes such as **split complementary** (three equidistant colors), **double-split complementary** (four colors made up of two sets of opposites), and the most complex of all, **tetrad.** Tetrad schemes are determined by placing either a square or a rectangle anywhere over the color wheel and seeing what four colors the device intersects. This scheme takes planning, but if you have a red sofa and love the idea of buttery yellow walls, you're halfway there.

This brings us full circle around the color wheel. So is there any combination that will not succeed? If you choose a color you love, add a dash of its complement, take a little risk with a painted piece here or there, and round things out with personal touches, the short answer is, "Probably not!"

Primary Colors

Secondary Colors

Double-Split Complementary Colors

Complementary Colors

Triad Colors

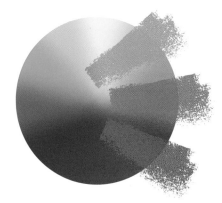

Analogous Colors

Split-Complementary Colors

the basic color palette

There are 14 basic colors you can use to produce almost any hue you need. There are additional colors, of course—well over 500, if you take into account all the different artist's media around the world. However, these 14 are the most common, and their names are standard in all the media used to create decorative paint finishes: universal tints, artist's acrylics and oil paints, and japan colors. Start with these 14, and add others as the number and complexity of your projects grow.

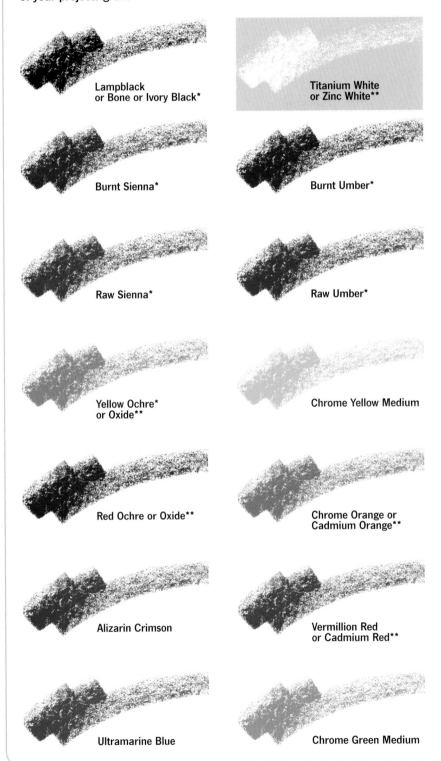

Lampblack
or Bone or Ivory Black*

Titanium White
or Zinc White**

Burnt Sienna*

Burnt Umber*

Raw Sienna*

Raw Umber*

Yellow Ochre*
or Oxide**

Chrome Yellow Medium

Red Ochre or Oxide**

Chrome Orange or
Cadmium Orange**

Alizarin Crimson

Vermillion Red
or Cadmium Red**

Ultramarine Blue

Chrome Green Medium

be a pro

PIGMENT SAFETY
A number of these pigments are considered toxic and must be handled with great caution. Poisoning can occur if paints with these pigments are inhaled or ingested. Highly toxic pigments include raw and burnt umber; cadmium red and orange; chrome green, yellow, and orange; and vermillion red. Alizarin crimson, lampblack, and zinc white are considered slightly toxic. When working with these paints, avoid eating, drinking, or smoking; use a dust-mist respirator when sanding or mixing dry pigments; and never use household containers or utensils to mix paints.

*These are the basic native colors that give you great control in neutralizing or toning down colors.
**Basically the same color; the pigment listed first is the less expensive of the two.

Note that all these colors have medium values. It's most economical to use medium values because these can be used in a number of projects, as they are easier to either lighten or darken with a dollop of additional paint.

reducing intensity with native colors

Name: Yellow ochre

Color: Medium dull yellow

Effects: Reduces intensity of true yellow; neutralizes purple and red-purple; adds yellow to and dulls the intensity of greens; turns black green; warms other colors.

Name: Raw sienna

Color: Medium dull yellow-orange

Effects: Adds pink orange to colors, including white; dulls the intensity of yellow; neutralizes blue and violet.

Name: Burnt sienna

Color: Dark red-orange

Effects: Neutralizes blue, blue-green, and green; gives other colors a warm red-orange cast.

Name: Raw umber

Color: Dark-value green-based gray/brown

Effects: Turns most colors grayer and darker; neutralizes red-violet and red; adds green to other colors; makes good grays when mixed with black and white.

Name: Burnt umber

Color: Dark reddish brown

Effects: Neutralizes blue; makes warm grays when combined with black and white; turns other colors warm and dark.

Name: Lampblack

Color: Darkest value native color; contains blue; a cool color

Effects: Cools and darkens all colors; neutralizes orange, red-orange, and yellow-orange.

be a pro

WITH YELLOW

Yellow will swallow up every ounce of blue daylight in a room. That's why that pretty yellow color you just painted the living-room walls looks green. So here's the deal: always take the color card outside and look at it in natural light when you're selecting a yellow. Bring a green reference chip along so you can see this tendency at work. Yellow is equally sensitive to artificial lighting. Incandescent bulbs (yellow light) enhance the tone; add a fluorescent (blue) light to the mix, and oh boy, you've got a real mess. (Halogen bulbs are whiter and closer to natural light than the two other types mentioned.) Avoid greenish yellows, and choose a shade that looks less intense than the final result you are seeking. For the best result, select yellows that are more buttery or honey-toned than you think you might like, trust me.

color consult...yellow

Sunshine and buttercups, cheerful and bright; a classically styled yellow room is splendid indeed. Yellow appears to be a perfectly reliable little color, much loved by architects and designers alike. Not to be a spoilsport, but keep in mind that yellow is also the color of construction equipment and used internationally for danger signs. Most yellow troubles are a product of its depth and reflective value, which also make it the easiest color for the human eye to see. If you find your lovely bright yellow room a little too intense, especially if you need to relax, consider adding a painted enhancement instead of a full-on redo because yellow can settle down quickly, as the example in "Tone It Down," on the next page shows.

tone it down

Yellow is such a happy color, no wonder parents often choose it for a child's room. But when the shade is too bright, the color may be overstimulating. How to tone it down without repainting the entire space? Add a gray dado in a simple stripe (below). If you're inexperienced with painting stripes, check out Chapter 6, "Pattern...Panache for Pennies," page 112.

- Install a stock chair rail 42 inches from the floor. An option is to paint a chair rail-inspired border in white to visually divide the wall surface. Prepare the room for a quick project; wash and sand the existing paint; and tape the trim.
- Using 1-inch blue painter's tape, mask off a pattern of wide vertical stripes over the existing vibrant yellow paint below the chair rail. Here, I applied the tape every 12 inches. You'll have to measure the width of your wall and, combined with the width you choose for the stripe, determine how many rows you'll need. You can cheat a bit here and there on a stripe's width to even up things.
- Apply two coats of a warm gray paint. Make sure the paint's finish is consistent with that of the existing yellow. Remove the tape promptly, pulling it toward the wet paint.
- Touch up the trim and bleeding as necessary using a wet rag. Then enjoy your now toned-down classic yellow room.

A SPIRITED PAINTED SUNRISE greets the room's young occupant and brightens up the entirely wood-clad space. It doesn't take much to completely change the personality of a room and get everyone smiling in the morning.

THESE WALLS WERE PAINTED A LOVELY PINEAPPLE YELLOW, which turned out looking like garish cadmium yellow. A golden yellow-brown brushed grass-cloth effect was applied, and the new sundrenched Naples yellow walls lived happily ever after with the cobalt blue and white furnishings.

color consult...green

It's so easy to live with green, and because it "goes" anywhere, it's practically a neutral. Green is what designers call "a friendly color," which means that there is hardly a design scheme that can't include it to a greater or lesser extent. Let green soothe your color apprehensions, and use it with confidence in unexpected places. Green looks awfully fabulous with purple, and it lives best with every shade of its complement, red.

A PAINTED CANOPY OF VIBRANT KELLY GREEN (right) adds a dramatic burst of fresh color to this simply furnished room. Let that be a lesson: the right choice and application of color can transform space.

GREEN can be quiet and soothing, too. This sleepy green is perfect for the nursery (left).

green's a natural

Some designers use green in the same way as a neutral (beige, brown, or white). Take the case of new, standard builder's doors. Giving them a coat of green, applied in a refined dragging technique, instead of painting them a bland off-white makes even the most inexpensive doors look special.

- Mask the hinges and hardware with blue painter's tape. If there is existing paint, sand the doors using 220-grit sandpaper, and then wipe them down with a clean tack cloth.
- Prime the doors; then apply two coats of soft blue paint. (I used an oil -based primer and base coat. If you prefer to work with latex paint, use an alcohol-based primer followed by two coats of semigloss paint that has been formu-lated for doors and trim.)
- Once dry, sand the base coat lightly using dry 400-grit wet/dry sandpaper. Then thoroughly wipe down the doors with a clean tack cloth.
- Prepare a latex glaze consisting of 2 parts glaze, 1 part water, and 1 part semigloss latex polyurethane tinted with cobalt blue. If you find that the glaze is too thin, add 2 teaspoons of blue acrylic craft paint to enhance the body. The glaze will be vivid and transparent.
- Brush the glaze onto the doors' inside panels, following the grain. Remove any excess glaze with a dry chip brush, and soften the look with cheesecloth. Let it dry. If you're concerned about damage, apply an isolating coat of clear shellac (shellac thinned by half with denatured alcohol).
- Mix a green clear-tint latex glaze. Use 2 parts glaze, 1 part water, and 1 part semigloss latex polyurethane tinted with an avocado or grass green. If you find that the glaze is too thin, add 2 teaspoons of a blue-green craft paint to enhance the body. This type of glaze should be vivid and transparent also.

- Brush the glaze onto the doors' rails and stiles, following the gra-in. Remove the excess glaze with a dry chip brush, and soften the effect with cheesecloth. Let it dry.
- Apply a protective topcoat of var-nish or polyurethane.

be a pro

WITH GREEN

As a mix of yellow and blue, green is balancing act of warm and cool. If you're thinking of painting a wall green, getting the right shade can be tricky—are you aiming for a cool minty hue (has more blue in it) or a pale olive (has more yellow in it). To be on the safe side, if you're trying to match a particular object or fabric, take it along with you to the paint store.

be a pro

WITH BLUE

Blue's flighty nature and ambiguous ways settle down when you introduce colors such as earthy cinnamon, gold, magenta, black, and white to the scheme. They ground complex blue schemes beautifully. Furniture pieces, both modest and grand, will look swell when you paint them carefully, and then drag an old-fashioned blue glaze over them. Make a sample board to experiment with a green, gray, or black base coat for your blue pieces.

BLUE IS ALMOST EVERYONE'S FAVORITE COLOR, but it has many moods. In a bedroom, above, a medium tone creates a restful ambiance.

ACCENT BLUE WITH YELLOW. These two colors are almost opposite on the color wheel. Yellow sunflowers add a cheery note in this kitchen (right), but you could use pottery, too.

color consult...blue

IF YOU DON'T LOVE GREEN, then you are surely "a blue person." When you are planning a design in blue, bring your paint colors and swatches on every shopping adventure. Blue, more than any other color, confounds visual memory. If you've been wrong about a blue again and again, take heart: most of the visual references everyone uses for it (ice, water, sky, robin's eggs, delphiniums) are ever-changing and elusive colors as well. This may be the very reason a perfectly executed monochromatic blue scheme is so fabulous—it's not quite as effortless as it looks.

pick-me-up blue

There's nothing like color to update or change a room. But when there's no money in the budget for more than a few gallons of paint, who cares? Fresh, new colors are sometimes all you need to pull off a fabulous new look, as demonstrated by this kitchen makeover rendered in a cottage-inspired palette. For added charm and vintage appeal, I painted the cabinets in a lime wash-style finish.

- Remove the doors—with the hardware attached—from the cabinet boxes. (Number each door, and prepare a written reference before removing them.) Mask the hardware.
- Sand the doors, shelves, and cabinet boxes with 220-grit sandpaper. Wash the cabinets inside and out with trisodium phosphate (TSP).
- Carefully mask the inside edges of the drawers and cabinet boxes.
- Apply a latex primer. Follow that with two coats of semigloss latex paint in white. Dry-sand the cabinets lightly between coats using 400-grit wet/dry sandpaper, and then wipe them with a clean tack cloth.
- Mix a blue latex glaze consisting of 2 parts latex paint and 2 parts glaze thinned by 50 percent with water. Apply the glaze to the cabinet boxes, following the grain. While the glaze is still wet, drag a dry brush through it to reveal the white base coat. Follow the same process on the doors.
- Thin flat white latex paint, using 1 part water to 1 part paint. Load a clean brush with the thinned paint; wipe it out on a paper plate or a board; and then dry-brush all of the surfaces with what's left on the brush. This will create a dry, powdery finish on the doors. Do not apply polyurethane or any other topcoat to maintain the dusty, slightly aged look of the lime wash-style finish.

USING CONTRASTING COLOR to draw attention to a nook or niche is an easy decorating trick. In this darling girl's room (above), blue makes an appearance inside a built-in bookcase. The small, light-blue polka dots can be dabbed on randomly using a round sponge.

Before

RED MIXED WITH WHITE results in delightfully feminine pink. Unlike a light blue or light green, pink deserves its own designation. Some pinks are cool (left) while others are warm.

FUNNY LITTLE PIECES seem to have an affinity with happy-go-lucky red. A table (below), with it's warm pinkish coral-red glaze is no exception.

BIG COLORS ARE BIG COMMITMENTS and orange (opposite top), which falls between red and yellow, is B-I-G. Support it with strong architectural features, and make sure it does not clash with colors in neighboring rooms.

color consult...red

SATURATED REDS fall into the category of "demanding." While unquestionably spectacular, red walls swallow up every drop of light because the color has a very low reflective value. Try a red feature wall if your room is too small for the whole treatment, or get out the red high-performance enamels, and then fix yourself up with a few unexpected red accessories. Even tiny bursts of red have a similar effect when it is pure, vivid, and bright.

be a pro

some red razzmatazz

A small "extra room" is often overlooked, especially if it's tucked away from the main living areas in a house. That's a perfect case for going red, which is what I did in the once-spare space that is now a welcoming guest room (right). When you are glazing a wall with red, use a base coat that is near what I call a "violent magenta." With red, the glazing process is a messy deal, but always worth the bother.

- Prepare the room for a messy job. Remove or completely cover the furniture, and mask all the trim. Protect the floor with plastic sheeting.

- Apply a latex primer. Let it dry, and apply your chosen shade of red.

- Mix a latex glaze that consists of 4 parts glazing liquid, 2 parts water, and latex paint. For a more purple-like red, add some blue latex paint into the mixture. Brush it onto the wall, and let it dry thoroughly if not overnight.

- Mix a scumble glaze that consists of 4 parts glazing liquid, 6 parts water, and a purple-gray tint that you can make by mixing the red and blue latex paints with a little black. Test it. If it's too dark, add a little white latex paint to it. Using a well-wrung wet rag, apply this overglaze to the wall, and soften your work with a brush. Work quickly because latex paint dries fast!

BLUE-GRAY VIOLET, or lavender, looks pure and clean in utilitarian spaces. There is no fresher color for a laundry room (opposite top left), and when mixed with yellow or orange, its more cheerful disposition really shines.

A FRIENDLY AND FRUITY PLUM COLOR enlivens this family room (opposite right). Aqua blue and granny-apple green add happy accents.

ADD SPARKLE TO A PURPLE ROOM to elevate the drama and richness of this color. Crystal and gold-tone accents shimmer brilliantly against the deeply saturated hue (opposite bottom).

punch it up with purple

A bunch of mismatched furniture styles can look cheap and uninspiring. But sometimes you have to live with what you've got. My recommendation is to start by painting everything white, and then go with a dramatic color on the walls. Here, powerful purple walls visually support the cohesive all-white rescue.

- Prepare the room for a big mess. Using a sanding pole for extra traction, sand the walls hard with 200-grit sandpaper, and then clean off any dust.
- Mask the ceiling line and all the trim with burnished blue painter's tape. Using a a putty knife, screwdriver or other dull tool, score all the taped edges well so that the paint floats to a sharp edge.
- Cut in the primer, which has been tinted in the paint department to as close to the finished color as possible, using a good-quality brush. With the best roller cage and cover you can afford, apply one coat of latex primer to the rest of the wall surface. (Tinted primers take longer to dry; double the drying time that is recommended on the label.)
- You'll need enough paint for two coats and a little extra. Combine all of it in a 5-gallon-size bucket, and stir it well.
- Cut in the ceiling and trim with a brush, and come down the wall surface twice as wide as you might otherwise do, perhaps a full 8 or 10 inches, to allow the first coat of paint to float to the scored and taped edge. Don't overwork the paint, and always lay off with the brush toward the direction of the light source.
- Roll the paint onto the rest of the surface—always working toward the natural light source—in a zigzag pattern: from top to bottom to top, and then up to and over the cut-in areas.
- Apply the second coat in the same manner. When everything dries, remove the tape, pulling it at a severe angle toward the painted surface.

be a pro

A highly saturated color, such as purple, requires precision when you paint with it. Also, be sure you have enough paint for the job before you begin. Computers and exacting paint-industry standards aside, super-saturated colors never mix the same way twice.

color consult...purple

POOR PURPLE. It is a very complicated color, and sadly, extremely underused. Purple, like brown, elicits a robust love/hate response: it can appear dull or theatrical, and of course, the funeral connotations don't help. Still, pale, gray-, and blue-like versions of a full-spectrum purple are really quite lovely and can lift a dull palette into the design stratosphere—if you're willing to take a chance. It's a gutsy color that lives surprisingly well with blue, green, pink, beige, yellow, gold, brown, and white. What more could you ask from a color? Give poor purple a chance, and go bold; it is truly an important color, which has been dismissed by the design community for far too long.

a Stroll down

general information about

the Paint Aisle

paint and paint-related products

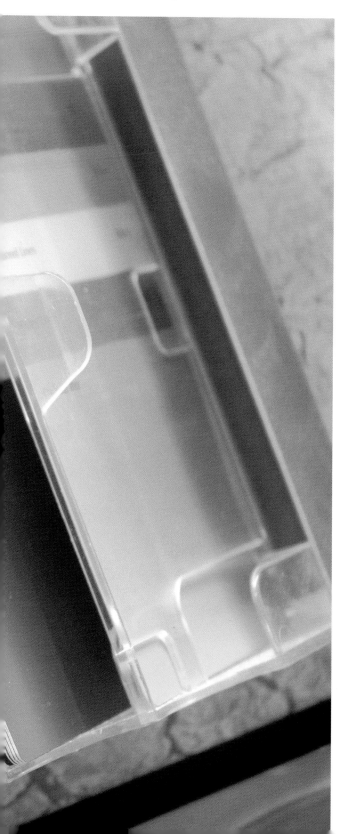

So many fabulous painting projects are the result of sensible experimentation combined with **serendipity**. Sometimes in the wild world of the decorative arts, not only can a paint "failure" turn out to be exactly **the look** you wanted after all, but there can be several forks in the road—and any one of them can lead to success. Whether your successful outcome is a happy accident or the result of **exacting application** of technique, choosing stable, **reliable products** for the job is a major factor. Beyond that, it's important to have a general knowledge of **solvents, formulas, dry times, appearance**, and an understanding of the attributes of paint products.

PAINT CHIPS GALORE await your arrival. Although color may be your muse, there are important things to know about paint and its related products as they apply to your decorating project.

Primers

This first, preparatory coat may be an oil- (alkyd), water- (latex), or shellac-based (alcohol) formulation. Choosing the right one for the job depends on what you will be priming and how you will be finishing the surface. I suspect each manufacturer's wish to convey their product's superiority for the task makes for all the confusing language associated with primers. Certainly myriad surfaces, situations, and scenarios exist for which one particular product may be better suited than another. While it might be interesting for me to speculate about each and every possibility, it's better that I do some decoding, after which you'll have the confidence to make your own decision.

alkyd (oil-based) primers

The term "alkyd based" is used interchangeably with "oil based" throughout this book and the painting industry. This is technically incorrect because they are not exactly the same. But for our purposes, using them this way, as most people do, is fine. Both are solvent-based products. I use the term "solvent based" interchangeably with "mineral spirits," "white spirits," and "paint thinner." The short story is an alkyd-based primer is an oil-based formulation that has been thinned and cleaned up with paint thinner or mineral spirits, and best suited for the priming of

- old existing paint, which may contain lead.
- shiny surfaces.
- radiators, painted metal, or any metal surface subject to rust.
- new or raw wood doors, medium-density fiberboard (MDF), trim with knots or tannins, anything plastic, hardboard, fine furniture, and fine wood cabinetry.

Alkyd primers dry slowly, sand beautifully, and accept any type of top coat as a finish. You can roll them onto a surface with a short-nap roller or brush them on using a natural bristle brush. Today, you can find alkyd primers that contain low levels of volatile organic compounds (VOCs), which are safer for you and for the environment.

RESTORING A VINTAGE STAIRCASE **often means dealing with lead paint. Not to fret; apply an alkyd primer before sanding and painting it.**

latex (water-based) primers

"Latex" is a term used interchangeably with "water based." This type of primer cleans up with soap and water, generally does not have as unpleasant a smell as other primers, dries quickly, and can be recoated soon—usually after only two hours. Latex primers will raise the grain of raw wood. They should not be used on any metal subject to rust (such as radiators) or on walls that are dirty or nicotine- or water-stained. A water-based formulation is best suited for the priming of

- new drywall.
- previously painted wall surfaces.
- previously painted unwaxed interior floors.
- ceilings.

Latex primers can be recoated with any latex paint, milk paint, artist's acrylics, and low-VOC products. Sand them with mesh or aluminum-oxide sandpaper.

alcohol (shellac-based) primers

Alcohol primers are nothing more than tinted shellac, which is a natural product made from the excretions of the lac bug. Shellac is a superior sealer, has excellent adhesion properties, will not raise the grain of open-grain woods, and sands beautifully. Quick to dry, a little runny for applying to walls, and a bit tricky to clean up later, alcohol primers are still very useful, but there's a catch—the fumes. You will need a lot of ventilation, and you should get all the children and asthmatics out of the house. However, the fumes don't linger, and any existing odors from tobacco, cooking grease, even fire and smoke damage, for example, disappear afterwards. A shellac-based primer is suitable for the priming of

- walls that are in very poor and dirty condition.
- recoating surfaces with existing oil-based paint.
- furniture.
- anything requiring excellent adhesion requirements, such as counters, tile, vinyl, linoleum, metal, plastic laminate, and even glass.
- new or raw wood doors, medium-density fiberboard (MDF), trim with knots or tannins, plastic anything, masonite, fine furniture, and fine cabinetry.

Alcohol primers dry quickly, will accept any top coat formulation, alkyd or latex, and sand beautifully. You can apply them with a very short-nap roller or use a brush that you should keep reserved for use with shellac products. (Use denatured alcohol to clean the brush.)

sealers and undercoats

Sealers, which are available in alkyd, latex, and alcohol formulations, have superior stain-blocking ability and are excellent for walls subject to water, dampness, or mildew. They have superior "hide" and can be tinted, making them good for walls you want to make dark or to thoroughly cover existing saturated colors.

Before beginning your project, be aware that sealers and undercoats smell like crazy no matter what their formulation. However, these products dry quickly and take a good sanding. Specifically formulated to seal, they are also the best bet for covering old wallpaper, porous surfaces, crayon, pencil, or walls that will not come entirely clean. Because sealers are a great product to stabilize unevenly porous wall surfaces, they also provide the best substrate for fine glazing techniques. I find them indispensible on very high walls, shower ceilings, and bathroom walls; in unheated spaces such as porches; and in other interior situations where the climate of the room is extreme or unusual.

specialty faux-finish products

DEPENDING ON WHERE YOU SHOP and the part of the country where you live, there can be anywhere up to 15 different "ready-made" paint and faux finishing products on display for every project, from Venetian plaster to crackle glazes. This is plenty for your experimentation. In fact, often these products perform unintended miracles when manipulated or combined with other techniques. There are a number of gadgets, fancy tools, and expensive specialty brushes in this section, as well. However, you won't need most of them.

Paint

All paint, no matter its specific formulation or chemistry, is made of three essential ingredients: pigment, binder, and vehicle. Why do you need to know this? So you will remember to stir the paint!

Sure, better manufacturers use higher-quality pigments that provide better hide and, yes, 100-percent acrylic paints are bound in a different vehicle than the resins used for a solvent-based paint. But once you open the can, all of this information is somehow irrelevant. Stirring the paint, blending the three ingredients, is the important thing. Without doing it, the sheen of a high-gloss paint will be uneven, oil-based paint may never dry, dark colors will dry patchy, and less-expensive vinyl resins will form little bumps on your walls. There are more paint failures associated with this seemingly petty step that, as it turns out, is of paramount importance. So, ask for the sticks—and always stir the paint!

sheen

Each type of paint, both alkyd and latex, is available in a variety of sheens or finishes. The language for this is beginning to change, as many new "green," products (low or no VOCs) are matte, which is a relatively new concept and term in the paint community. For the purpose of covering a wall surface, and assuming I am speaking of proprietary paint sold in quarts or gallons, the word "sheen" is a reference to shine or reflective value as well to the paint's porosity. The terminology may vary somewhat from one manufacturer to another, but for interior paint products, the following finishes are currently available. (Specialty paint products are discussed beginning on page 187.)

High gloss. This is the least-porous and shiniest paint finish available. High-gloss enamels are shinier than high-gloss latex paints, and high-gloss oil paint is the shiniest of them all. This sheen will call attention to every imperfection in the surface, but it can be incredibly beautiful under the right circumstances. It has a lot of "slip," making it unsuitable for any type of glazing other than a strié or dragging technique, but it looks awfully terrific on fabulous millwork. To ensure an even shine once the paint or finish dries, stir high-gloss products often.

Semigloss. A durable finish, semigloss is not very porous. It's a good choice for doors, trim, and furniture, and as a base coat for most glazing techniques, with the exception of stone and color washing. It's a matter of opinion whether semigloss is a good choice for a wall finish, and

depending on the brand, it will appear shiny and call attention to imperfections. I find semigloss paint sometimes peels when it's used on a floor, but it looks good on furniture pieces. Semigloss paint will also crack a little and sometimes peel if it's used over vinyl, melamine, or most surfaces primed with an alcohol primer. Instead, flat paint proves more suitable for these applications.

Satin. With about half the sheen of a semigloss finish, satin has more sheen than eggshell. As washable as its shinier counterparts, this finish is available in a low-VOC formula and makes the most sound base coat for most faux finishes and glazing techniques. Satin finishes are lovely on their own, look smart on furniture, and do not peel as much as semigloss sheens. Available in alkyd and latex products, it's a nice all-round, go-anywhere finish.

Eggshell. This finish is the best bet when you're working in a dark color. It's nearly flat, but not quite. With a little bit of side sheen, eggshell helps lift a very dark color, which can sometimes look dull in a flat finish. Eggshell finishes make good grounds for paint techniques when neither porosity nor shine are desired, but they do have some slip. It's a good compromise for a color-washing base coat when you need time to work across a large expanse of wall. However, not every manufacturer offers an eggshell finish.

Flat. Flat paint is a go-anywhere, do-everything product. The lack of sheen, particularly when flawlessly applied in multiple coats, is nearly as washable as a mid-sheen product, and has the added benefit of concealing imperfections in walls and ceilings better than any single paint product on the market. I prefer flat latex paint for painted floors, color-wash base coats, stone-finish base coats, and unusual painting projects when there is some question as to what product is best for the job. I can't remember the last time a flat latex has let me down, nor can I remember the last time I had the good fortune to work in a flat oil, which is nearly a thing of the past, and will require a good deal of tenacity to find.

be a pro

DROP CLOTHS
Rolls of plastic are handy to cover furnishings and isolate a room. Invest in heavy drop cloths for the floor; they don't slip underneath your feet. The long, narrow drop cloths are the best for around a room's perimeter; they are easier to fold than the giant ones, and they are less of a hassle to wash and store.

MY COLLEC-
TION OF
STIRRERS can attest to
my many
years of
experience
restyling and
restoring almost
everything with
paint.

product compatability

Use this quick reference guide to select products with the same solubility. Products with the same solubility successfully combine with one another whether you're mixing them together or layering them on top of one another. Usually, you'll have to separate those with different solubilities from one another by applying an isolating layer of shellac or varnish. Shellac is not listed here because it is alcohol-soluble and may be used as an isolating layer between both water-soluble and solvent-soluble products.

WATER-SOLUBLE	SOLVENT-SOLUBLE
UNDERCOATS	
Polyvinyl acetate (PVA) sealers	Alkyd sealers
Latex primers	Alkyd primers
PAINTS	
Latex interior paints	Alkyd interior paints
COLORANTS	
Artist's acrylics	Artist's oil paints
Universal tints	Universal tints
Casein	Japan colors
Tempera	
GLAZE MEDIUMS	
Transparent acrylic gel	Commercial oil glaze
Latex glazing liquid	Alkyd glazing liquid
THINNERS	
Water	Mineral spirits
	Paint thinner
	Turpentine
	Boiled linseed oil
TOP COATS	
Acrylic varnish	Oil varnish
Water-based polyurethane	Polyurethane

*Do not intermix products with incompatible solvents.
*Do not intermix compatible paint products with incompatible sheens.

solvents and thinners

In every paint store, there exists a mysterious little section stacked with interestingly colored cans containing solvents, the names for which are growing increasingly unfamiliar. There are a few things worth checking out and fewer still you may actually need. Be sure to always read the labels on solvents, handle them with care, never mix them together unless you have a degree in chemistry, and store them safely, knowing that in case of fire, it is not a good idea to have an attic full of accelerants.

Mineral spirits and paint thinner. There's not too much of a difference between paint thinner and mineral spirits other than cost. Essentially a processed petroleum product that's used as a solvent for oil-based products, paint thinner, the more expensive of the two, may be intermixed by the manufacturer with other solvents—most likely naptha, which will not alter its performance in any meaningful way or change its relatively fast rate of evaporation.

Odorless and low-odor paint thinners are more expensive alternatives to mineral spirits and generic paint thinner. They all perform the same function—thinning, cleaning, and hastening, somewhat, the dry time of oil-based products. They all produce fumes and are flammable, but they're a necessary evil. Just remember, they will knock the shine out of a gloss product. I prefer mineral spirits because the fumes are, for me, the most familiar and least offensive.

Denatured alcohol. This is the solvent to use with shellac and shellac-based primers. It thins shellac by as much as 50 percent for a spit coat, which is a thin "primer" for shellac. Clean brushes with it after applying a shellac-based primer. Denatured alcohol evaporates very fast, so keep it and whatever product you add it to covered.

Naptha. Sometimes substituted as a solvent for mineral spirits or paint thinner, naptha will clean paint, brushes, and tools quite nicely. You can also use it to safely remove spilled or splattered paint from a surface, such as a floor, glass, furniture, and so forth, without disturbing the finish.

Boiled linseed oil. A nice product for conditioning the bristles of your good brushes, the wood handles of your best brushes, and metal tools and blades. It will keep your brush-cleaning tools from getting rusty; especially if they live in the water bucket as do mine. I spread it around the top of my most prized cans of oil-based paint so that they close tightly and open easily.

Added to an oil glaze, boiled linseed oil will also extend the "open time," and add a great deal of body to the glaze. You can also add a little bit to paste wax, shoe polish, and wood putty to rejuvenate and emulsify these products.

Lighter fluid. Nothing removes the sticky residue left by tape, pricing stickers, or labels like lighter fluid. It will not disturb the finish on appliances, plastic, sinks, bathtubs, vinyl, ceramic, or wood floors. It only takes a drop on a rag or a scrubbing pad. But do not use it on marble.

Brush cleaner. While this is a costly product, and unnecessary if you maintain your brushes, it is still a good thing to have on hand. There's nothing worse for a dedicated painter than discovering a favorite sable brush rock hard under a drop cloth, and then realizing there is nothing at hand with which to clean it.

Use this water-wash formula after you have cleaned your brushes, giving them one swish, followed by a final wash. If a brush gets away from you, brush cleaner will usually soften hardened paint enough for a rescue—with some doing. It makes quick work of caked ferrules or bristles that have dried together and the annoying residue good primers leave in synthetic brushes. Stored covered in a metal can, the useful clean stuff that remains in this liquid will rise to the top in a day or so, after which you can pour it off into another clean container to reuse it later. Then swirl the goop out of the bottom of the can for disposal.

More Stuff

The patching and covering-up section of the paint store will get your hair standing on end, so keep it simple. Buy the best caulking gun you can find; caulk that contains paintable silicone; lightweight joint compound to patch drywall; wood putty; and window glazing putty or wood filler to cover small nail holes. That's it.

Tools such as patching blades, painter's guides, putty knives, mud pans, hawks, and other items are each available in high-quality metal or inexpensive plastic. If you are planning a lifetime of patching and filling, buy metal. For a one time quick fix, plastic, which is actually easier to clean, will do the trick. Oil your metal blades from time to time to keep them in good order and rust free.

UNIVERSAL TINTS let you create your own custom hues and try out different color combinations.

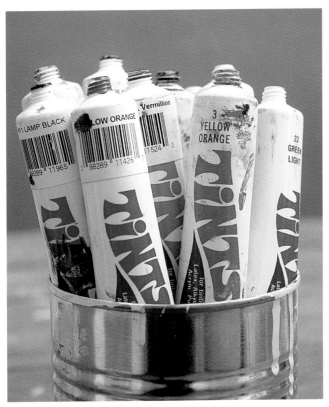

A BASIC SET OF COLORANTS is kind of like an old favorite from childhood—the "big box" of crayons. Start by purchasing a few and gradually expand your collection.

Specialty Paints and Colorants

Last time I checked, some 3,000 companies were in the business of manufacturing paint and of these, each manufacturer offers well over 2,000 colors. Add to that modern computer technology, which can produce a color by matching nearly anything, and the need to mix (I'm not talking about stirring paint) a color even comes into question.

Proprietary premixed color is reliable and consistent; the paint is available in various formulas and sheens; and who needs all those messy little tubes hanging around, you might ask? Well, sometimes the color is a little too bright, or a little too hot, or just a little too pale.

Then there's the issue of all the leftover paint; what will happen if you dump this yellow into that green? The result: a decent blue for the bathroom—maybe. A modest collection of universal tints will prove indispensable for mixing glazes, and discovering how to mix or adjust a color with a drop of black or a dash of red will save you time and money.

While there is more to know about color than any single

book could ever teach, taking the time to master a few basic color-mixing skills will be invaluable to your painting exploits and a real boon to your ego when you begin to get it right every time. Soon you may discover that besides a yellow-ocher tint, you must have chrome yellow, cadmium, Indian, Naples and yellow oxide, too. Good color instincts can be developed quickly through trial and error, and once you gain an understanding of how to arrive at a specific hue, the daunting task of selecting from those tiny little paint chips will become less overwhelming.

An inexpensive watercolor set and a bit of white latex paint will keep you busy for some time, and it's a great way to fool around with combinations. Or you can assemble a basic set of universal tint colorants to mix and build your confidence. (See Chapter 9, "Solve It with Color," page 164, for a full list of universal tints.) Start by purchasing a few, and then expand your collection.

Universal tints can be combined with any oil-base, latex, or acrylic paint, polyurethane, varnish, Japan paint, and Venetian plaster. That's why they're called "universal." Increasingly difficult to source from local paint dealers and home centers, you can find them online. (See the Resource Guide on page 192 for a list of distributors.) Some manufacturers offer complete starter sets, generally in a larger size than the more familiar small tubes. These tints create more saturated colors, which are useful in Venetian plaster and larger quantities of paint. The cover is attached to the bottle of the larger size colorants, making them easy to find and to close tightly. They dry quickly if left uncovered, and some are toxic. Read the labels, and wear gloves.

Japan paint. Japan paint is sold in most quality art-supply stores in quarts and half-pint sizes. Used by sign makers, oil-based Japan paint has excellent leveling qualities, sands like glass, mixes well with colorants, and dries quickly. It also mixes well with oil-based glazes, and it's a superior product for furniture, making it worth the bother of handling and clean up after using it.

Milk paint. Literally made from milk, this is a super environmentally friendly, essentially latex product. Milk paint dries dead flat. It is a bit chewed up in appearance when you use it on furniture, but polyurethane will take care of that. Great for projects when the kids are involved, it's sold in many beautiful colors. Its very dry appearance makes it a great latex-formula mixing glaze for color washing.

Artist's oils and acrylics. Sold in tubes or small containers at art suppliers and craft stores, these are the real deal. Their full range of colors is unbeatable. They can be tinted, made into glazes, used for small projects, or for tinting or mixing colors. You'll need a palette or paper plate or plastic tray of some sort to work from, but don't put too much out at once; acrylics dry up very quickly. Keep your brushes clean as you go. The tube oils can be quite costly, owing to their authentic pure pigments, and some are toxic.

Craft paints. You will love this stuff. Sold in small bottles at all craft shops, it is available in oodles of interesting, accurate, saturated colors. These paints are easy to use and easy to clean, and they come in lots of reliable sheens, as well as metallic and pearl finishes. In addition, they're inexpensive.

While fine faux finishers may scoff at the idea of using craft paints for stencils, furniture, painting fabric, or on floors, all I can do is recommend it. They have only one drawback: they are not good for mixing glazes. I own and use them by the bagful, and they store exceptionally well upside down. Craft paints can be sanded lightly and re-coated easily; they dry quickly; and they are entirely stable when protected by polyurethane, varnish, or shellac. Test clear spray finishes, which may cause some crazing.

Enamel. There was a time anything labeled enamel meant a shiny oil-based product modified with varnish. Today, enamel is a code word for "hard." There are oil-based, latex, high-heat, rust-inhibiting, and high-performance enamels. All dry relatively hard compared with other paint products, but more importantly, they adhere well and have exceptional hide. While it may be the quality of the finely ground pigment or the chemistry or ratio of binders in the paint itself, either way it is a terrific product. Use oil-based enamel on radiators—latex will encourage rust. I'm happy to report I have found low-VOC, latex high-gloss enamels in gallons. (See the Resource Guide on page 192.) It is a superior green alternative to oil-based paint for cabinets and furniture.

Sandpaper

You can still buy sandpaper in individual sheets at a good hardware store and mixed packages at a home-improvement

MILK PAINT is an excellent choice if you want to re-create the look of American Colonial furniture or painted walls and floors. It's made from the same natural ingredients—milk, lime, and earth pigments—that were used to make milk paint in the eighteenth century.

center. It is also available in precut shapes that fit on a sanding block or wall sander. You will find you can never have enough sandpaper once you start using it.

I have never intentionally thrown away a piece of sandpaper in my entire career. I keep all shapes, sizes, and grits in a big box. Buy the purple or red garnet paper to use on raw wood, the brown aluminum oxide paper for general purposes, the black silicone carbide wet/dry paper for fine sanding, and the green production paper, which never seems to wear out, for heavy work. Sandpaper performs best on furniture when you use it with a sanding block; for sanding a wall, use a sanding pad.

You'll find the sandpaper's grit noted on the back of the sheet, 60-grit being the heaviest, or most abrasive, 80, 100, 120, 150, 180, and finally 220 grit, which is the most commonly used one for general purposes and walls. You can use black silicone carbide closed-coat sandpaper, really an emery of sorts, wet or dry. It's available in up to 1200 grit for fine sanding; 240, 320, 400, and 600 grits are good for working with varnish and polyurethane—adding a little soap to the

water when you're using this sandpaper wet will enhance the shine of the finish.

Sanding mesh and sponges are useful on unpainted joint compound. Big wall-sanding projects will require the swivel-pole sander head to affix the mesh and a sanding pole.

There remain a few old timers who perform the most elaborate process to ready a piece of sandpaper for use—rubbing the paper onto itself; folding it in half precisely; running a painter's 5-in-1 tool down the fold to cut the paper; and finally, folding the remaining half sheet into thirds. It's a dance worth doing; sandpaper is getting expensive, and it deserves some respectful handling for all the messes it can remedy and fine results it guarantees.

Glazing Liquid

Glazing liquid can be oil-based, which is thinned and tinted with oil-based products and solvents, or water-based, which is thinned and tinted with latex products or water. Use compati-

TWO IMPORTANT TOOLS are sandpaper, which comes in different grits, and a broad knife, which is necessary for working with joint compound.

ble paint products with them, or use universal tints.

Each manufacturer's glazing liquid differs a little bit from the next in terms of drying, viscosity, transparency, and "open time," which refers to the time just before the paint dries when you can still manipulate it. Open time is the most critical issue effecting most glazing projects, and there are additives that can be mixed into the media to extend or prolong the drying time considerably. An oil formula, now sold only in quart quantities, stays open much longer than latex. (See "The Classics," on page 12, which explores extenders, additives, and recipes for mixing a glaze.)

Reuse, Recycle, Save

There remains a long list of supplies you may want on hand for a big painting project. If you have a good deal of work to do, shop around and accumulate them a little at a time. Start saving old coffee and soup cans to use for mixing, take-out containers for palates, empty spackle buckets for cleaning brushes and storing things, and large-mouth glass jars. Professional painters and decorative artists are a thrifty gang, owing to the ever-increasing costs of buckets, store-bought rags, and petroleum-based products in general. Here is a quick list of some cost-saving ideas.

- Buy old shirts and towels from the neighborhood thrift shop. You can use them for glazing and cleanups. Save old dish towels and bath towels. Cotton sheets and worn-out flannel are excellent for polishing wax and for Venetian plaster projects.
- Save the containers from packaged meats to use as palettes, to hold screws and hardware, or for small spray-painting projects. Aluminum restaurant "doggie bag" containers with plastic tops offer two palettes for the price of sweet and sour chicken.
- Hang on to all those short pieces of wood the carpenters throw away to prop furniture up off the floor or for painting color samples. Grab all the long, thin pieces of wood to use for stirring.
- Plastic spoons, paper plates, small plastic cups, inexpensive foils and wraps, buckets, and sponges are but a few things that cost much less at the dollar store.
- Inexpensive plastic table cloths, old or low-cost plastic shower curtains, unwanted fabric curtains, big pieces of cardboard, and small pieces of carpet turned upside down all make perfectly useful cover-ups and drop cloths.
- Save the tops from every paint can; they make good color

mixing palettes. Use the empty paint cans as buckets or to store supplies. They are also handy for remixing paint.
- At the paint store, always ask for a few extra stir sticks, try to get a box, and insist your dealer give you the well-hidden and much-coveted long stick if you buy paint in 5-gallon quantities.
- Save old nylon stockings and sheer or lace curtains. Use them as paint or polyurethane strainers. Save odd socks for cleaning brushes and little rags for tiny drop cloths.
- Shoe boxes are great for keeping a small container of paint, a tack cloth, sandpaper, and a dusting brush in one place when traveling around with the tiny dropcloth to paint baseboard, trim, furniture, or cabinets.
- Newspaper is the single best thing to clean off brushes; old magazines and junk mail also do fine.
- Hang on to those annoying little plastic bags—they can keep a brush dry while you're having lunch. You can also use them to temporarily cover mixed paint and glaze containers. Better-quality plastic bags will line a standard-size roller pan perfectly. Be sure any print is on the inside, away from your fresh paint; slip the pan into the bag; loop the handles over the feet; and you'll never need to clean a roller pan again.
- Dry-cleaning plastic is perfect for so many things, you will never throw it away again. The same is true of loose paper packaging and tissue paper.
- Hang on to old toothbrushes for scrubbing tools.
- Plastic packaging that zips, the sort that come with curtains or linens, is great for storing razor blades, glues, universal tints, tiny cans that won't close completely tight and may spill, markers, and measuring tools.

There are a few things you may only find at the paint store. Some are more necessary than others, and the list is in no particular order.

- For cleaning, keep a metal comb, wire brush, brush cleaner, brown bar soap, fabric softener, and buckets on hand.
- For safety, make sure to have masks, gloves, goggles, and a fire extinguisher.
- For measuring, acquire a measuring tape, ruler, chalk-line box, level, square, plastic triangle, and pencils.
- For cutting, have scissors, razor blades, a craft knife, carpet knife, and box cutter on hand.
- For decorative finishes, collect assorted sponges, cheesecloth, rags, chamois, steel wool, wallpapering brushes, squeegees, and graining tools.
- For cleaning, get buckets, vinegar, dishwashing liquid, tack rags, a vacuum cleaner, dusting brushes, a dust pan and and brush, and powdered, heavy-duty trisodium phosphate (TSP).

resource guide

The following list of manufacturers and associations is meant to be a general guide to additional industry and product-related sources. It is not intended as a listing of products and manufacturers represented by the photographs in this book.

MANUFACTURERS & DISTRIBUTORS

UNITED STATES

Acme Sponge & Chamois Co., Inc.
800-937-3222
www.acmesponge.com
Distributes natural sponge and chamois products worldwide.

Addicted to Rubber Stamps
www.addictedtorubberstamps.com
Sells rubber stamps, paper crafts, and related products.

Allerdice Building Supplies
518-584-5533
www.allerdice.com
Distributes paint and paint supplies.

Behr
800-854-0133
www.behr.com
Manufactures paint, varnishes, and related products.

Benjamin Moore & Co.
800-344-0400
www.benjaminmoore.com
Manufactures paint, stains, and varnishes.

Bestt Liebco Corp.
800-547-0780
www.besttliebco.com
Manufactures painting tools, such as brushes and rollers.

Chroma
717-626-8866
www.chromaonline.com
Manufactures art supplies.

Colker Co.
800-533-6561
www.colkercompany.com/decorative_arts.html
Manufactures natural sea sponges and cloths.

DaVinci Paint Co.
800-553-8755
www.davincipaints.com
Manufactures artist's paints, brushes, and knives.

Delta
800-423-4135
www.deltacrafts.com
Manufactures paint, stamps, and stencils.

Dick Blick
800-828-4548
www.dickblick.com
Sells acrylic, ceramic, fabric paints, universal tints, and art supplies.

Dunn-Edwards
888-337-2468
www.dunnedwards.com
Manufactures paint and related materials.

Fine Paints of Europe
800-332-1556
www.finepaintsofeurope.com
Manufactures fine brushes, brushing putty, and alkyd paints.

Glidden
800-454-3336
www.glidden.com
Manufactures paint and related materials.

Grumbacher
800-628-1910
www.grumbacherart.com
Manufactures conventional oil and water-soluble oil paints.

Houston Art, Inc.
800-898-7224
www.houstonart.com
Manufactures metallic powders, thinners, and other art supplies.

Jamestown Distributors
800-497-0010
www.jamestowndistributors.com
Distributes high-performance alkyd paints and other supplies.

Jerry's Artarama
800-827-8478
www.jerrysartarama.com
Distributes sponges, crombs, graining tools, and specialty supplies

resource guide

J.W. Etc.
361-887-6600
www.jwetc.com
Manufactures varnish, wood filler, and opaque primer.

Loew-Cornell. Inc.
866-227-9206
www.loew-cornell.com
Manufactures artist's brushes and accessories.

Magically Magnetic
724-352-3747
www.lyt.com
Manufactures magnetic paint.

Mannington
www.mannington.com
Manufactures tile and other types of flooring.

Mark James Designs
www.markjamesdesign.com
Manufactures wall decals.

Masterchem Industries
866-744-6371
www.kilz.com
Manufactures varieties of primer.

Minwax
800-523-9299
www.minwax.com
Manufactures wood stains and high-performance fillers and finishes.

Olde Century Colors
800-222-3092
www.oldecenturycolors.com
Manufactures paints and varnishes.

Palmer Paint Products
800-521-1383
www.palmerpaint.com
Manufactures paint products for general craft purposes.

Pearl Paint
800-451-7327
www.pearlpaint.com
Distributes a wide range of fine-art products, including paints and brushes.

Plaid Industries
800-842-4197
www.plaidonline.com
Manufactures craft-related products, including paints, stamps, and stencils.

Pratt & Lambert
800-289-7728
www.prattandlambert.com
Manufactures paint, stains, and other related products.

Purdy Corp.
503-547-0780
www.purdycorp.com
Manufactures brushes.

Ralph Lauren Paint
888-475-7674
www.ralphlaurenhome.com
Manufactures metallic paint.

Sheffield Bronze Paint
216-481-8330
www.sheffieldbronze.com
Manufactures universal tints.

Sherwin-Williams
216-566-2284
www.sherwin-williams.com
Manufactures paints and finishes.

Solo Horton Brushes, Inc.
800-969-7656
www.solobrushes.com
Manufactures artist's and utility brushes.

3M
888-364-3577
www.3m.com
Manufactures sandpaper and other products.

T.J. Ronan Paint Corp.
800-247-6626
www.ronanpaints.com
Manufactures specialty paints.

U.S. Art Quest
800-766-0728
www.usartquest.com
Manufactures art supplies, including paints and adhesives.

Valspar Corp.
800-845-9061
www.valspar.com
Manufactures paint, stains, and coatings.

Victoria Larsen
425-258-6812
www.victorialarsen.com
Manufactures stencils, stencil-making supplies, and
plaster molds.

West River Natural Paints
www.westriverpaints.com
Produces low VOC, natural old fashioned paint.

Winsor & Newton
800-445-4278
www.winsornewton.com
Manufactures artists' paints.

Zinsser Co, Inc.
732-469-8100
www.zinsser.com
Manufactures wallcovering-removal products, primers,
and sealants.

CANADA
General Paint
888-301-4454
www.generalpaint.com
Manufactures paint, architectural coatings, and wallpaper.

Nour Trading Co.
800-686-6687
www.nour.com
Manufactures professional painting tools.

Para Paints
800-461-7272
www.para.com
Manufactures paint, stains, and varnishes.

FAUX FINISHERS

Artistic Designs by Deidre
518-475-7973
www.adbydeidre.com
Fine artist and faux finisher.

Esmond Lyons
518-307-5929
elyons3@nycap.rr.com
Decorative and fine-art painter.

ASSOCIATIONS

UNITED STATES
American Craft Council
212-274-0630
www.craftcouncil.org
An organization that offers educational workshops
and seminars to the public.

Craft & Hobby Association (CHA)
201-794-1133
www.hobby.org
Offers information, projects, and tips.

CANADA
Canadian Craft and Hobby Association (CCHA)
403-770-1023
www.cdncraft.org
Promotes growth for its members through education.

Canadian Crafts Federation
905-891-5928
www.canadiancraftsfederation.ca
A national organization that represents Canadian
craft councils.

glossary

Accent color. Contrasting color used in small proportions to draw the eye and add interest.

Acetate. The plastic sheet material used for cutting stencils.

Acrylic. A water-based plastic polymer that acts as the binder in acrylic paints.

Acrylic varnish. A coating that contains the same medium used to make water-soluble paints and glazes.

Advancing colors. The warm colors. As with dark colors, they seem to advance toward you.

Alizarin crimson. One of the basic pigments, alizarin crimson is synthetically derived from coal tar and ranges from scarlet to maroon.

Alkyd paints. Paints with artificial resins (alkyds) forming their binder; often imprecisely called "oil-based" paints. Alkyds have replaced the linseed oil formerly used as a binder in oil-based paint.

Analogous colors. Any three colors located next to one another on the color wheel.

Antiquing. Any technique used to make a painted surface look old; usually refers to a thin glaze that is applied to a surface, allowing the undercoat to show through.

Artist's acrylics. Paints that contain pigments suspended in acrylic resin, similar to latex paint but of much higher quality.

Artist's brushes. Fine-tipped brushes for intricate work.

Artist's oils. The tube or oil-stick paint associated with fine-art paintings. They consist of pigments suspended in linseed oil.

Base coat. The first coat of paint, which seals the surface.

Binder. A viscous, pliant material that holds pigments in suspension and makes them adhere to surfaces—the bulk of what makes up paint.

Blender brushes. Specialty brushes used to blend and soften all types of wet surfaces.

Boxing. Pouring all paint of the same color and formula into one large container and then mixing it together to eliminate minor variations in color between cans.

Burnt sienna. One of the native colors, this is a deep, rich rust-red made from calcined raw sienna.

Burnt umber. One of the native colors, burnt umber is a dark reddish brown made from calcined raw umber.

Breccia marble. Marble that is composed of sharp fragments cemented together.

Cadmium orange. One of the basic pigments, cadmium orange is made from cadmium sulphide and cadmium selenide.

Casein paint. An old-fashioned paint made by mixing pigments with milk solids. It is seldom used except on furniture where a faded look is desired.

Cheesecloth. A loosely woven cotton gauze used to create many different textures as well as to blend and smooth all techniques.

Cheesecloth distressing. The process of blending and softening paint strokes and colors by pouncing bunched-up cheesecloth over the wet surface.

China bristles. Another term for bristles made from boar hair.

Chroma. See Intensity.

Chrome green. A variety of green pigments made from chrome yellow and iron (Prussian) blue.

Chrome orange. One of the basic pigments, this orange-red pigment is made from lead chromate and lead oxides.

Chrome yellow. One of the basic pigments, this yellow pigment is made from lead chromate combined with lead sulfate.

Clear top coat. A transparent finishing layer of protection applied on top of a painted finish.

Color scheme. A group of colors used together to create visual harmony in a space.

Color washing. Random layers of thin glaze that are blended to produce a faded, uneven look similar to that of whitewash or distemper.

Color wheel. A pie-shaped diagram showing the range and relationships of pigment. The three primary colors are equidistant, with secondary and tertiary colors in between them.

Combing. Any paint technique that involves marking narrow lines of color on a surface. Also called "strié" or "dragging". Combing techniques that specifically intend to imitate wood are called "wood-graining" techniques.

Complementary colors. Colors located opposite one another on the color wheel.

Contrast. The art of assembling colors with different values and intensities to create visual harmony in a color scheme.

Cool colors. The greens, blues, and violets.

Crackle glaze. Water-based glaze used under paint to create a peeling effect.

Cutters. Short, stiff-bristled brushes used to cut in lines, such as in corners and around trim.

Decoupage. French term for the technique of pasting and varnishing paper or fabric.

Deglossing. Roughing up a surface before painting so that it has "tooth," a texture that grabs paint.

Distemper. An old-fashioned type of interior paint made with a casein or gelatin/glue-size binder.

glossary

Distressing. Imitating wear and tear by rubbing down.

Dragging. See Combing.

Dusting brushes. Soft, medium-length brushes used for combing, stippling, and softening textures.

Earth tones. The natural colors of earth; browns and beiges.

Eggshell. A thin, brittle semi-matte paint finish.

Enamel. Paint with finely ground pigments and a high binder content so that it dries to a hard gloss or semi-gloss finish.

Faux. French for "false"—used to describe any technique in which paint imitates another substance, such as wood or stone.

Ferrule. The metal part of a paint-brush that attaches the bristles to the handle.

Flags. A word describing bristles with split ends, which help hold the paint.

Flogging brush. Wide, long-bristled brush used to texture surfaces by dragging or slapping wet paint or glaze. Also called a dragger.

Frieze. Lateral band decorated differently to the rest of a room, usually high on a wall.

Gilding. Decorative technique giving a metallic appearance.

Glaze. A paint or colorant mixed with a transparent medium and diluted with a thinner compatible with the medium.

Gloss. A shiny finish that reflects the maximum amount of light.

Graining combs. Flexible steel or plastic combs that come in a variety of sizes and are used to striate and grain surfaces.

Grit paper. Also called "sandpaper"—an abrasive paper used to smooth surfaces.

Harmonizing colors. Neighboring colors on the color wheel.

High-gloss finish. Paint with a shiny finish, usually oil-based.

Heart grain. Wood with a V-shaped grain pattern.

Hue. Synonym for color. Used most often to describe the color family to which a color belongs.

Intensity. The brightness or dullness of a color. Also referred to as a color's purity or saturation.

Intermediate colors. Colors made by mixing equal amounts of one primary and one secondary color, such as red-orange and blue-green.

Japan colors. Concentrated oil-based colorants that are used for tinting alkyd paints and solvent-soluble glazes. Japan colors have an intense, flat color and will dry quickly.

Jasper. An opaque form of quartz that is usually yellow, brown, red, or green.

Lacquer. Protective clear finish, applied in several thin coats.

Lampblack. One of the native colors, lampblack is a deep black made from nearly pure carbon (containing some oil and tar impurities).

Latex paints. Paints that contain acrylic or vinyl resins or a combination of the two. High-quality latex paints contain 100-percent acrylic resin. Latex paints are water-soluble; that is, they can be thinned and cleaned up with water.

Leveling. The ability of a paint to smooth out after application so that it shows no brush or roller marks when it is dry.

Liming. Decorative technique of applying liming wax to create a soft, aged-looking finish.

Lining brushes. Thin, flexible, long-bristled brushes that are used for fine lining and detail work.

Linseed oil. An oil derived from flax seed that is used in oil-based paints and varnishes.

Matte finish. Also called "flat"—a dull, unshiny finish.

Mineral spirits. A petroleum distillate used as a solvent for alkyd-based paint.

Morocco leather. A soft and expensive leather made from the skin of goats tanned with sumac; by extension, a paint technique imitating it.

glossary

Mottler. A flat-ended brush used to make textures in glazed surfaces.

Nap. A soft or fuzzy surface on fabric such as a paint roller cover.

Native colors. The basic inorganic pigments derived from pigmented earth colored by minerals and used to make the basic colors found in artist's oil paints: burnt sienna, burnt umber, lampblack, raw sienna, raw umber, and yellow ochre.

Negative technique. Any decorative painting technique that involves removing paint from a surface while it is still wet. See Positive technique.

Oil-based paint. Hard-wearing paint made from alkyd resin

Oil varnish. See Varnish.

Overglaze. A thin glaze added as a final step to a decorative finish. It can be the original glaze thinned somewhat or a new, thinner glaze in another color.

Overgrainers. Long, flat-bristled brushes used to apply paint detail, generally on dry, previously grained surfaces.

Palette. Set of colors in a scheme.

Palette knife. An artist's knife with a dull, flexible blade, used for mixing paints on a palette.

Parchment. An animal skin used for writing or paper made in imitation of it; by extension, the decorative finish that has a similar appearance.

Pastel. A color to which a lot of white has been added to make it pale in value.

Pigment. The substances that give paint color. Pigments are derived from natural or synthetic materials that have been ground into fine powders.

Polyurethane. A plastic resin, which makes a good top coat for most types of paint except artist's oils. Thin it with mineral spirits or with water if water-based polyurethane.

Positive technique. Any painting technique that involves adding paint to a surface, which creates more depth. See Negative technique.

Primary colors. Red, yellow, and blue; the three colors in the visible spectrum that cannot be broken down into other colors. In various combinations and proportions, they make all other colors.

Primer. A coating that prepares surfaces for painting by making them more uniform in texture and giving them tooth.

Ragging off. The technique in which paint is pulled from a surface using a bunched-up cloth. Sometimes called "cheeseclothing."

Ragging on. The technique in which paint is applied to a surface using a bunched-up cloth.

Rag-rolling off. A technique in which paint or glaze is removed from a surface using a rolled-up piece of cloth that is lifted off in a rhythmic pattern.

Raw sienna. One of the native colors, raw sienna is an earthy yellow-brown made from clay containing iron and aluminum oxides, which is found in the area of Tuscany around Siena.

Raw umber. One of the native colors, raw umber is a cool brown made from a clay containing iron oxides and manganese dioxide, originally from the Italian region of Umbria.

Receding colors. The cool colors. They make surfaces seem farther from the eye.

Red ochre. One of the basic pigments, red ochre is a red tinged slightly with violet, made from clay containing iron oxide.

Refined white beeswax. Derived from natural beeswax, this product produces an elegant, lustrous finish that doesn't yellow.

Registration marks. Small holes cut into a stencil with more than one layer, which allow you to match up the different layers.

Resin. A category of solid or semi-solid, viscous substances, both natural (rosin, amber, copal) and synthetic (polyvinyl, polystyrene).

Round fitches. Round brushes with firm but flexible bristles. They are used for spattering, stippling, and stenciling.

Rust inhibitors. Chemicals added to special paints intended for metal surfaces that may corrode.

Satin finish. Paint finish that is mildly

shiny with little glare. Also known as "semigloss."

Sealer. A product (for example, shellac) that seals porous surfaces by forming a durable, nonabsorbent barrier that prevents them from sucking up paint.

Sea sponge. The fibrous connective structure of a sea creature used to apply and remove paint. Not to be confused with the cellulose variety used in household chores.

Secondary colors. Orange, green, and volet; the colors made by mixing equal amounts of two primary colors.

Semigloss. A slightly lustrous finish that is light reflective and has an appearance somewhere between gloss and eggshell.

Shade. A color to which black has been added to make it darker.

Sheen. The quality of paint that reflects light.

Shellac. The secretion of a Southeast Asian insect dissolved in alcohol, which is used as a sealer. It comes in three colors: clear (sometimes labeled "white"); white-pigmented (also referred to as "opaque" and "chalked white"), and "orange," or "blond."

Snap time. The point at which a paint or glaze has begun to dull down and become tacky. After snap time, a paint cannot be worked without causing damage to the finish.

Solvent. A liquid capable of dissolving another substance (such as mineral spirits for alkyd paint and water for latex paint).

Spalter. A type of natural-bristle brush used for smoothing on alkyd paints.

Spattering. The technique of applying random dots of paint over a surface by striking a saturated brush or rubbing paint through a screen.

glossary

Sponging. A paint technique that uses a natural sea sponge to apply or remove paint.

Staining. Technique of using oil- or water-based paints to add transparent color to wooden surfaces.

Stencil. A cut-out pattern. Complex stencils will have several overlapping patterns, and different colors are applied in layers after the previous coat dries.

Stippling. A paint technique that involves pouncing a special brush straight up and down over a surface, creating myriad tiny dots that blend together when viewed from a distance. Similar to the fine-art technique known as "pointillism."

Stippling brush. A blocky, stiff-bristled china brush used to stipple wet paints, glazes, and top coats.

Strié. See Combing.

Tempera paint. A mixture of pigments and a water-soluble glutinous emulsion binder, often made from an oil extracted from egg yolks.

Terebene dryer. A substance (prepared from oil of turpentine) that can be added to alkyd-based paints (most often house paints) to speed drying.

Spattering. Decorative technique to spray dots of paint onto a surface.

Texturing compounds. Substances that go into paints where a rough, grained, or dimensional quality is desired.

Thinner. A liquid that is mixed with paint to make it less thick, such as turpentine or white mineral spirits for alkyd-based paints and water for latex-based paints.

Tint. A color to which white has been added to make it lighter in value.

Titanium white. The most common white pigment, titanium white is a brilliant white that is synthetically derived from the metal titanium.

Tonal value. The lightness or darkness of a color.

Tone. A color to which gray has been added to change its value.

Tooth. The coarse quality of a surface (or a coating on a surface) that improves the performance, appearance, and longevity of paint.

Triad. Any three colors located equidistant from one another on the color wheel.

Trompe l'oeil. French for "fool the eye"—used to describe a painted surface that convincingly mimics reality.

Turpentine. A solvent made from distillate of pine resins, used as a thinner and cleaner for alkyd-based paints.

Ultramarine blue. One of the native colors, ultramarine blue is an intense blue originally made from crushed lapis lazuli, but now formulated from man-made pigments.

Undercoat. Protective layer of paint between primer and top coat.

Universal tints. Pigments that are combined with ethylene glycol and a small amount of water. They are usable in both water- and alkyd-based paints and glaze mediums.

Value. The lightness (tint or pastel) and darkness (shade) of a color.

Value scale. A graphic tool used to show the range of values between pure white and true black.

Varnish. The traditional top coat used in decorative painting, consisting of an oil-based paint with a solvent and an oxidizing or evaporating binder, which leaves behind a thin, hard film.

Vehicle. See Binder.

Vermillion red. One of the basic pigments, vermilion red is a brilliant pure red made from mercuric sulphide.

Visible spectrum. The bands of hues created when sunlight passes through a prism.

Warm colors. Generally, the reds, oranges, and yellows; often including the browns.

Wash. A thinned-out latex or acrylic paint.

Water-based polyurethane. A sealer made from polyurethane resins that is water- rather than oil-soluble.

Wavelength. The means of measuring the electromagnetic spectrum; the portion of this spectrum that is visible as light has waves that measure between 4,000 and 7,000 angstroms, with red having the longest waves and violet the shortest.

Wet edge. A margin of wet paint or glaze. Leaving a wet edge creates a seamless blend between sections.

Wood graining. A painting technique that seeks to resemble wood by imitating the lines or growth rings found in cut lumber.

Wood stain. A translucent combination of solvent (either water- or alkyd-based) and pigment, usually in colors imitating natural wood, which allow some of the wood's natural color and its grain to be visible.

Yellow ochre. One of the native colors, yellow ochre is a mustard-yellow made from clay containing iron oxide.

Zinc white. A common white pigment, it is brilliant and derived from the metal zinc.

index

index

photo and designer credits

All photography by Mark Samu & all designs by Lucianna Samu, unless otherwise noted.

page 2: design: Lee Najman Design, Inc.
page 11: design: Artistic Designs by Deidre
pages 12–13: design: Grey Advertising
pages 14–15: *center* design: Mercedes Courland Design
page 29: design: Vanguard
page 33: *top* design: Artistic Designs by Deidre
page 34: design: Grey Advertising
pages 35–36: design: Gretchen Agans Design
pages 54–69: design: Artistic Designs by Deidre
pages 92–93: design: Lee Najman Design, Inc.
page 103: design: Hearst Magazines
page 106: *top* design: Noli Design; *bottom* design: Keith Baltimore Design
page 107: *top* design: Bonacio Construction/Tom Frost AIA
page 108: design: Patrick Falco Design
page 111: design: Anne Tarasoff Design
page 114: *bottom right* design: EJR Architects
page 118: design: The Michaels Group
page 119: *right* design: Steven Goldgram Design
page 126: design: EJR Architects
pages 132–133: design: Ragozzino Interiors

page 134: *bottom* design: Artistic Designs by Deidre
page 135: design: Ragozzino Interiors
page 139: design: Artistic Designs by Deidre
pages 144–145: design: Artistic Designs by Deidre
page 146: *top* design: Artistic Designs by Deidre; *bottom* design: Ragozzino Interiors
page 147: design: Artistic Designs by Deidre
pages 148–149: design: Artistic Designs by Deidre
page 154: design: Beach Glass Design
page 158: *bottom* design: Carolyn Miller Interiors
page 159: design: Pascucci Deslisle Design
pages 164–165: design: Donald Billinkoff AIA
page 170: design: Charles Reilly Design
page 171: *bottom left* design: Artistic Designs by Deidre; *bottom right* design: Healing-Barsanti Design
page 172: *bottom left* design: Artistic Designs by Deidre
page 173: Artistic Designs by Deidre
page 177: *top* design: Charles Reilly Design
page 179: *top right* design: Charles Reilly Design
page 198: design: Ragozzino Interiors
page 201: design: Anne Tarasoff Design
page 202: design: Gretchen Agans Design
pages 206–207: *left* design: The Michaels Group; *right* design: Noli Design

Have a home gardening, decorating, or improvement project?
Look for these and other fine **Creative Homeowner**
books wherever books are sold

Natural Style
Over 200 color photos. 208 pp.;
8½" x 10⅞"
$19.95 (US) $21.95 (CAN)
BOOK #: 279062

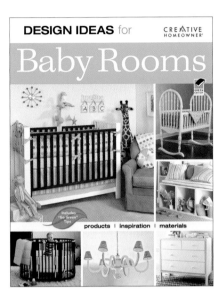

Design Ideas Baby Rooms
350 color photos. 208 pp.;
8½" x 10⅞"
$19.95 (US) $23.95 (CAN)
BOOK #: 279294

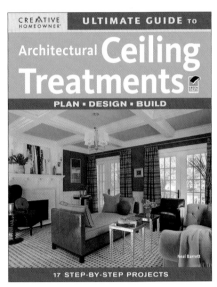

**Ultimate Guide to Architectural
Ceiling Treatments**
Over 530 color photos and illos. 192 pp.;
8½" x 10⅞"
$19.95 (US) $21.95 (CAN)
BOOK #: 279286

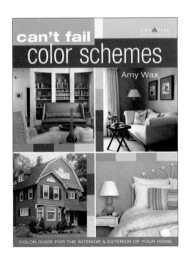

Can't Fail Color Schemes
300 color photos. 304 pp.;
7" x 9¼"
$19.95 (US) $24.95 (CAN)
BOOK #: 279659

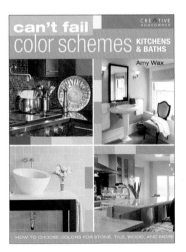

**Can't Fail Color Schemes
Kitchens and Baths**
300 color photos. 304 pp.;
7" x 9¼"
$19.95 (US) $21.95 (CAN)
BOOK #: 279648

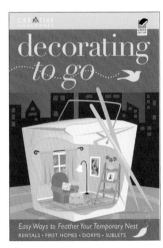

Decorating to Go
200 color photos. 176 pp.;
6¼" x 9¼"
$12.95 (US) $15.95 (CAN)
BOOK #: 279582

For more information and to order direct, go to **www.creativehomeowner.com**